Mother of the Year
and other
Elusive Awards
Misadventures in Autism

Fran

D1533870

KALYN FALK

enjoy!

I'm looking for a place to start, and everything feels so different.

- Just grab a hold of my hand, I will lead you through this wonderland.

Water is up to my knees and sharks are swimming in the sea.

- Just follow my yellow light and ignore all those big warning signs...

"Yellow Light," Of Monsters and Men

ACKNOWLEDGMENTS

This project began in one crystalline moment. I was being interviewed on TV, asked to justify why my child had jumped in the river, requiring a flotilla of police and inadvertent volunteers to save him. "Our house burned down six weeks ago, and we've had a lot of stress," I began. And, as I paused, wondering how to explain the fire, and the river rescue, and the fact that my son was smiling delightedly as he was wheeled away from the scene instead of looking deeply penitent and regretful, I could see my Mother of the Year Award slipping out of my grasp.

How can you condense a 14-year relationship with a profound diagnosis into a manageable sound bite? As my life with Noah flashed before my eyes, like a demented nightmare of a family brag book, I knew that it just didn't sound... like nomination material.

My son has become something of an urban legend in our city. Many people have met him (usually in the middle of a life threatening rescue scenario) or heard of him in stories that my husband tells in trainings.

I used to be the one that people knew.

But having children, especially one with a disability, has often cast me as a supporting player in my own life story. I have often been the voice that apologizes even when Noah is not penitent or the one who accepts people's assumption that I did something to cause his autism and that it is my job to find the solution. I am also the one to tearfully ask for government support even when I promise that we will do our best to make him less of a drain on the system in the long run.

It is time for me to find my own voice after spending so much time helping Noah find his. These are my stories, as much as they are Noah's. At least they are my attempt to find my own voice in the midst of a diagnosis that tries to speak on behalf of our whole family.

I am so grateful for my family, my husband and true love, David, and my manboys, Jase and Noah, for making space for me to write, and giving me plenty of fodder to work with. What would I do without you? I am especially grateful for my mom, Elvira Pain, who has been both catalyst and support to me, my sister Lisa Ryder Cohen who feeds my inner artist, and my cousin (sister) Catherine Bargen, who has been the midwife to this work, and has blessed me with her enthusiasm. And to Ana Hrynyk, my friend down the street who keeps popping up in my stories, who decided that autism isn't enough and added chemo to her plate. Thanks for walking this road with me.

I am also forever in debt to Noah's respite team, Laurel Epp, Laura Reis (and family!), Ryan Asselstine, and Sydney Bulmer—people who have taught me how to receive, claimed Noah as their friend and become my family. There are many other respite team members, health practitioners, educators and support service providers who have supported our family and many more to come. We're continually astonished at the quality of people who journey with us.

Special thanks to Lisa Ryder Cohen and Rachel Twigg Boyce for story editing, and especially to Catherine Pate for her encouragement and thorough text editing.

In my "real" job as a spiritual director, I am forever awed and humbled by the courage of my directees in sharing their sacred stories. Thank you for teaching me the power of vulnerability, claiming your voice and receiving love.

THE BOOK I WANT TO WRITE

Here's the book about autism that I want to write:

Our beautiful child was diagnosed with autism. Over the next three years, with tenacity, determination and the fierce love of a tiger mother, I fought the dread beast autism through *insert miracle cure here* and won. Now I praise God for the miracle of a perfect child and remember fondly those difficult three years, which made me a better person and taught me that, with enough love, faith and hard work, nothing is impossible.

I've read a few books like that, and believe me, I'd love to contribute to the field with my own hard work/dedication formula. But this is not my story. My story is more like:

Our beautiful child was diagnosed with autism. It shattered me. It overwhelmed our community and my faith. I've spent the last 12 years wandering through a lonely, subtle, complex universe where I've discovered deep beauty and truth, devastation, heartache and miracles. Autism has influenced every part of me. It's like cat hair in a Goodwill Store—I can't shed it. It has revealed my inadequacies as a mother and it has humbled me.

The truth of autism is that it is a neurological condition. A mother's love/will/courage will not rewire the brain, the same way that a mother cannot grow a new leg for an amputee or pray the acne away from a pubescent face.

The Mother of the Year Award (in my mind) goes to the person who not only has love/determination, but also gets results, and this is why my award has been lost in the mail for the last dozen years. My child, after years of intensive therapy, special diets, ridiculous amounts of herbal supplements, a service dog, and sincere prayer, remains functionally non-verbal and profoundly autistic. He is demanding and costly and can be a danger to himself and others. He is also hilarious, passionate, charming and a dedicated artist.

The book I want to write would make me look fabulous and you feel inadequate. However, autism has a way of writing its own story. It is not interested in heroes, villains or victims. It is more interested in looking at the story in unexpected ways. I hope it can be a companion to you if you're on a similar journey, or at the very least, provide an anthropological study of what it's like to live on a different planet.

EARLY WARNING SIGNS

One of the first things that people ask me when they find out that Noah is autistic is, "how did you know?" I'd like to think that this comes from an enquiring, scientific mind. However, since it is usually accompanied with worried eyebrows and the sense that the person listening is going through a mental checklist, I think people are looking for reassurance. OK, that sounds less and less like my child. A deep breath and sigh of relief often follow.

The funny thing is, our OTHER son was so intense (we called him Volcano Boy) that we were thrilled at how easy Noah was. He was also so incredibly fat (no one believes this, but it's true; he weighed thirty-two pounds at three months. I obviously lactate whipped cream. I sometimes think that I missed my calling and should have donated my breasts to science to provide for all of those two pound babies that need fattening up). We could sit him up at three months, simply because the size of his butt, combined with the rolls on his stomach, made him a human Weeble Wobble. Because his cheeks were so round, it was hard to see a lot of facial reaction or responsiveness.

Every parent has their own story, but I remember two "pings" of recognition long before the actual word "autism" came to mind. At four weeks old, I was giving Noah a bath and the scream he let out was the first indication—this is not a "wah wah" kind of baby cry. This is, if he had words, the filthiest kind of swearing directed at me. He was not sad. He was absolutely enraged. Normally he was the calmest, easiest baby, but bath time turned him into a mobster with a vendetta.

The next ping happened at about six months. I was holding him against my chest so he could look over my shoulder. A friend came up from behind and smiled at Noah and Noah simply looked away. No reaction or curiosity, just a shutting out. My friend said, "he reminds me of ____ (one of his nephews)" and I shot back, "No he doesn't!" without even thinking, because that nephew was odd and I recognized too clearly that Noah indeed, did remind us all of him.

At first I felt it most through the absence of connection or recognition. By eight months, he would not flirt with a camera, play hide and seek or look for toys if they fell from view. Soon the presence of strange behaviours added to the sense that something was off. When he started walking at eleven months, he would spend hours walking in circles around me. At about thirteen months, I was chewing bubble gum and he watched while I blew a big bubble and let it burst. The look on his face was one of horror and he immediately threw up. I realized that he wasn't necessarily aware that I was a different person from him—when he saw an enormous pink bubble come out of my mouth, he thought his insides were coming out of his mouth. (Being the kind, loving mother I was, I immediately replicated this as soon as my husband came home from work. "Get a load of this! Isn't this weird?" And Noah would do it twice more before he learned to toddle away the minute I brought out the gum.)

He would look sideways at objects with lights. We thought he might be deaf because he didn't respond to us calling his name, but his whole body shook with delight when he heard the theme song of Veggie Tales. He seemed only deaf to human voices.

Around thirteen months, he started having seizures to deal with anger or pain. He would go rigid and his eyes would roll back, then he'd shake for about ten seconds and then go limp as a rag doll and be unconscious for a few minutes. It was around this time that we started getting familiar with the people of 911. By the time the ambulance would come, Noah would be fine and we'd enjoy a $250 ride to the hospital only to be sent home again—he never had the lingering listlessness, the loss of bladder control that would have indicated a grand mal seizure. We started accumulating a pile of white teddy bears with a paramedic outfit—a thoughtful gesture by the paramedics who gave the bears to kids who might be scared. Noah didn't care about them, but I asked for one each time we went for a ride—for $250, you ask for every single perk you can find.

The seizures were not "medical" ones—they were labeled, "breath-holding two"—kind of like the super intense version of the kids who hold their breath until they pass out. This was a child who could not handle feelings of pain or anger and had learned a way to shut his body completely out of the experience.

He didn't do anything that was typically autistic—he didn't line toys up, didn't bang his head, didn't walk on tiptoe. But there was a sense that he wasn't living full time on our planet. And the grocery list of weird little things, combined with the seizures, started to tell a story of a very different way of being in the world.

As doctors began to believe me that we needed to define what that difference was, Noah went through a 7-month process of testing. There is no test to prove autism—just a series of tests to prove that he didn't have anything else. So we found out Noah was not blind, not deaf, not fragile x, not epileptic, not genetically challenged in any way. Really, it should have felt like a series of victories—all of the ways that my child is NOT outside of the pack! However, it felt like a slow circling around the inevitable, a series of hoops designed to prepare you for the final day when the label is given.

The actual day was a bit anti-climatic. The doctors I dealt with were all lovely, conflict avoidant people. They were extremely hesitant to label or define. I finally said to the neurologist, "I think it's autism" and he said, "Well, that's obvious. But I'd like to find out why." In that moment, I think he forgot he was talking to the mother of the subject and let me follow him down to his main interest; what caused the autism? What separates this subject from the others?

I did not, and still do not, really care why it happened. I just wanted to know what I was dealing with. After that meeting, I told each doctor that the neurologist had given the label and they were happy to concur with a diagnosis that had already been spoken.

Now when I'm with a baby, I go through the series of secret tests. I can't help it. The checklist is implanted in my mind. Makes eye contact, check. Replicates facial movements, check. Reacts to objects and surprises, check. Astonishing. It is a miracle to see the little faces respond so naturally, no one having to teach these skills. No one having to break each of these skills down to manageable chunks to practice for months. No one having to reward these skills with candy to teach that they are positive experiences. I marvel at these little ones who breeze through the complex social demands, oblivious to their own genius.

THE EDGE OF THE HERD

There are some positive sides to autism. I'm not going to give examples because I can't think of any off the top of my head, but I'm sure that they are there.

In terms of the negatives, some are pretty easy to call to mind. First off, the whole grieving for the life you thought your child would have, the kind of parent you were going to be, the idea that having children would be easy and you'd be good at it. All of that needs to change, and fairly significantly.

Then there is the loss of dignity. You try looking cool and blasé while you apologize to people at McDonald's while your child eats their fries. When your child runs naked into a public swimming pool while you chase madly after him (also naked). When your child stops a church service, wedding service, symphony in its tracks with a long primal scream. (Those are just hypothetical situations, if you've ever witnessed one of these events occurring, it WASN'T ME.)

Autism most definitely takes away your seat at the cool kids table and places you squarely in the haggard, misfit section. The cool moms casually visit while their children entertain themselves in the playground, their children stand nicely at the choir concert without flapping their hands wildly. The parents of autistic kids look on with a sort of crazed hunger, unable to find their way into the exclusive club of normalcy.

However, over time, you are able to deal with it. Your expectations about life do change radically. And sometimes, you get glimpses into the deep truths of life. About what it means to be human, to be loved and loving in spite of imperfection. And the more you become aware of the misfits around you, the more you realize your mom was telling you the truth when she said that the interesting people are never the ones at the cool table.

But one thing that sucks about autism that I'm just beginning to understand is that it turns you into a traitor.

A mom's job, upon the birth of a new baby, is to protect and defend the newborn. To find a place for it in the centre of the pack so that it is safe. We teach our children to conform because it keeps our kids safe from the danger of being isolated, rejected or bullied. We herd them into the group. (I know, I know. We like to think we promote individuality, but even the way we celebrate our kids' "uniqueness" is still within the bounds of a collective sense of what is tolerated. That's why girls these days can be named Willow, but not Bertha. Or why hipsters rebel against conformity and all look the same in how they choose to do that.) We know what it feels like when the herd is culled, how devastating it feels to be found wanting.

But the mom of an autistic child is usually the first person to get a little niggle that something is not right. At the beginning, there aren't even words or concrete situations that can be described, just a feeling that something is off. Does a good mother point at her child and say, "something here is very wrong?"

When a mom bravely voices a concern, she's met by well-meaning friends and family who say, "he'll grow out of it," "don't worry so much." Doctors hedge their bets, saying it's too soon to tell, everything will be fine. What people want to say is "he's one of us," not knowing how far the apple has fallen from the tree.

This is the brutal price of autism. The mom must be persistent in pointing out the flaws, the inconsistencies. She must hold her child up and repeat "this isn't right." It's devastating. It's our animal instinct. Even a peahen will leave the nest and sacrifice herself to lead a predator away from her baby. And here we are, drawing attention to our own child's vulnerability. We can feel in our bones that we should be on our child's side, but we can't ignore the feeling that something is wrong. We betray our role. Our job is to be the one who comforts, who soothes, who says, "You're going to be fine. You are perfect."

We do not want to be the one who sings, "You will be farther from me than I can understand. You will face challenges that are beyond comprehension."

When the diagnosis comes, it is almost a relief. I'm not crazy. I have a name for what's going on. I knew it. Everyone praises you for catching it so early. You are a good mom for fighting for your child. The herd may even learn to rally around your child and protect his or her vulnerabilities. And you slowly learn to forgive yourself for your betrayal. For being the one who had to hand your child over to the wolves.

KEEPING THE GOOD GUYS IN

The first time I ever heard about autism, I was in the back seat of a royal blue Oldsmobile, making our weekly trek across town to church. I was about nine or ten. My older sister was describing a dream she had had the night before; a dream of her being a mom and having a child who was autistic. "Artistic?" I had asked and she corrected me. She told me autistic people were fairy children—different and tragic but sort of magical. I took this information in, enjoying learning a new word, rolling it around in my mind like found treasure. My sister's world was full of magic and I never knew if she was telling the truth. I remember holding on to that new word as we drove by the old school for the deaf, the building that looked like a castle and tucked disabled people neatly away from us.

In high school, I watched "Rain Man" and learned that autistic people are highly structured and can't handle stimulation. I also learned that they are geniuses at math and say funny things.

When I studied autism as part of my degree in psychology

at university, I learned that autistic people are usually retarded (we would use a different word now), unable to communicate, and often aggressive. Institutionalization was the unfortunate, but only solution for this serious condition.

I had to relearn what autism was when Noah was diagnosed. This was not a kid who lined things up or got overwhelmed by sound. And we never knew if he was rigid with structure because there wasn't a shred of it in our house his first five years. Noah would run over and lick the speakers when his favourite songs would come on. The only thing that would console him when he was upset was to walk with his fingers trailing on a chain link fence. David tried copying Noah on a walk and his fingers went numb after thirty seconds. Noah could do it around the entire perimeter of a school yard and was soothed.

"Rain Man" depicted a person who was hypersensitive; his brain amplified all sensory information so that a small sound would be perceived as intolerable, or a barely noticeable flicker of a fluorescent light would be wildly distracting and even cause headaches. Noah's brain is the exact opposite. He is considered hypo-sensitive. It's like he minimizes information, so he needs a lot of stimulation before anything registers. He loves sour candy, arm scratching, bright colours and music so loud that he can feel it in his chest. My tin can of a car has the radio jacked so the bass is maximized and the speakers are focused on the front right side so he can put his hand on it and feel the vibration. It makes us seem very gangsta, thubbity thumping along the street, bass booming, until we open the door and reveal the menacing bass as part of a Veggie Tales song, experimental Icelandic bands, or some angsty folk singer rather than the expected hip hop.

The way that Noah's hypo-sensitivity showed up most was in his need to run. I'm not sure if it was simply the deep pressure it brought to his joints, or if it sped up the environment enough to make things interesting, but the boy loved to run. In the early days, he was content to run circles around me. Then he started running back and forth in the house. In an effort to make his running more interactive, we installed a small mirror on the wall in the dining room so he would see his own reflection. He would spend hours running back and forth, slamming his hands and body into the wall in the living room, then turning around to hurl himself toward the mirror in the dining room.

He also loves jumping. When he was two we bought him a mini-trampoline and he was literally my bouncing baby boy. People walking by would often stop and watch, fascinated, by the bouncing boy in the window. Of course, the trampoline wasn't visible, so Noah's hopping looked pretty epic. He was the Energizer Bunny that wouldn't stop.

We have gone through a few trampolines since then, getting bigger and bigger to accommodate our growing boy. Now we have an industrial grade 14-footer outside. Last winter, Noah would spend two hours a day jumping, enjoying the snowballs forming by his feet as he jumped, delighted when David would join him and double bounce him, sending him six feet in the air, but content to bounce by himself as well. He smiles and does a cat purr/dolphin chirp kind of sound. Jumping and running to Noah is the same thing as chocolate, wine and Suduko for me.

By the time Noah was three, he realized that the funnest place to run was outside. I don't remember the exact timeline of his first escape, I simply have a series of details that are etched in my body's memory: the quiet click of the front door, the feeling in my stomach as we ran through the house checking to see if he was hiding somewhere, the growing panic as we called 911 and tried to figure out where he would go, the ache in my chest, arms stretching out for a baby who was out of reach, the sobbing as I stood on the sidewalk, completely powerless. David had gone off running to see if he could find Noah, but I was anchored to the house, feeling a need to be a connecting point. I willed the phone to ring, the universe giving me a clue to where Noah would be.

And the phone did ring. A family was driving across the bridge and saw Noah running by himself. They didn't recognize him, but knew he was from their neighbourhood and should not be alone. They bundled him into their car and took him home, terrified that someone would mistake their actions for kidnapping. Once he got to their place, he was delighted and ran through their house, jumping in their beds. They didn't know if he was deaf, or what his deal was. The oldest daughter had been to one soccer practice with our older son and thought she remembered that he had a jumpy brother, so they called the soccer coach who gave them our number. They called to say Noah was safe and they were bringing him over. I was so relieved and could barely wait to have him back in my grasp again. One thing the family that rescued him hadn't counted on was getting him back into the car though, so it took a little longer than we all thought to return him.

Since then, it has been an ongoing dance to keep our boy from disaster. He starts to run, we install locks and alarms on the doors. When he can reach the gate latch, David rebuilds the fence and turns the gates inside out so you

13

have to reach over the gate and undo a carabiner before the gate will open. When we open the door to check on him at night and find him climbing out the window, we replace his screen with a pegboard so he can't get out but can still get some ventilation. When he gets into paint, candy, lotion, or glue, we install locks on all the cabinets. When he starts obsessing about the colour blue and putting blue shirts over the lights, we get rid of any halogen in the house, remove all lamps and install potlights that won't get knocked over or covered. When we sleep in a hotel, we put a chair in front of the door and fill the chair with suitcases and hangers, so the clatter will wake us if Noah tries to get out. We had a medic alert bracelet made with our phone number and address on it so that Noah could be returned to us if he did get out. We also put a latch hook on his bedroom door, so he couldn't escape in the middle of the night.

We spent Noah's first nine years within arms reach of him at all times (or in reach of a respite worker). I stopped going to the bathroom if I was alone with him unless he came in the room with me. I still don't shower until he's gone to school. Our house started looking like a bunker with all of its locks and alarms, but our concern has always been to keep the good guys in more than the bad guys out. Sometimes this has been the difference between a near miss and a full-on calamity. It certainly has prevented a lot of extra calls to 911. But it is also just an illusion. It helps us feel that we've done everything that we can. Nothing can guarantee safety, though.

One time when David, Jase and Noah were in the backyard, Noah discovered that we had left the garage door unlocked and ran in, pushing up the metal door and escaping to the back lane. David saw it all happen and ran to the gate at the same time to cut him off at the pass, Jase following along behind. Of course, our gates are reversed and he had to wrestle over the door with the carabiner before getting to the lane himself, giving Noah a full ten-second lead. David has long legs and can usually catch Noah in a sprint, but Noah's endurance tops anyone in the family. I was inside and had heard David yell, so I dropped everything and ran out the front door, sprinting my way to the busy street half a block away, thinking he was heading for the bridge. Midway there, I realize that my panic might have paved the way for new disaster; David might have yelled, caught Noah and put him in the house, not realizing that I had left the front door unlocked as I ran down the road. I looked back and saw nothing. I looked forward and saw nothing. Looked to the side, saw my neighbours staring out the window at me, checking to see if I needed help. Embarrassed, I came back home, not sure what was happening. David and the boys hadn't returned, so I took the car out, in case they needed back-up. I drove to the major intersection ahead of us and saw Jase standing on the corner, crying. He had been chasing David, who was chasing Noah and couldn't keep up. We went a little farther and found David holding on to Noah, clearly shaken. Noah miraculously had run across the busy street just when the light had turned from red to green, so all the cars were at a standstill. The drivers apparently saw David running, because they waited for him to cross as well. The gap between boy and Dad was widening when a guy on a moped turned around to help David chase Noah. A woman jumped out of her van and the guy on the moped herded Noah into her arms. When David caught up to them, she offered a ride home but he was too rattled to recognize her as the parent of a friend from school and just wanted to get home without any more attention. He got back to Jase and me, and we drove home.

When I talked to my family services worker about Noah's escapes, she paused for a moment and then said, "Where were you when all of this was happening?" I tried to explain how it happens. How sometimes it happens when you can see him the whole time, you just can't keep up. How you might lean over to tie your shoe and he slips away, or you don't think it's worth it to shut down the TV show he's watching just so you can bring him upstairs to bring a basket of laundry up, so you think you're safe for thirty seconds. When we talk about Noah's misadventures, I hear the Family Services worker's question behind the concern: "Could you be doing more?"

We held on to Noah's hands whenever we were outside until he learned to squirm away. Then we held his wrists until they went red and we were scared of injuring them. We grabbed the back of his t-shirts and twisted them around our hands so that he'd stay with us and the shirts started falling to pieces. We put a belt on him and tethered it to our belts and people made fun of us for having our child on a leash. It was the only way to go out for a while. Then people starting asking "What is it that he's running from?" wondering if he was so unhappy with us that he had to flee. My nostrils are flaring even now as I write this. No. He does not want to get AWAY from us. He loves to run. He needs to run. His brain does not comprehend safety. He is living in this present moment and has no fear, no sense of how this makes us feel.

He does not yet understand what it feels like to be scared, to know that he is alone, to be in pain and learn that there are consequences to impulsive actions—not until later. For now, there is only joy in running, in feeling wind and speed and excitement. Only peace knowing that angels will bring him home, protected from all harm.

SIX STAGES OF GRIEF

1. Denial
Luckily for me, the medical team in charge of diagnosing Noah expertly handled this initial stage of grief. One stage down, five to go. That's what team work is for, non?

2. Anger
There is no right way to respond to someone whose child has just been diagnosed. But believe me, there are PLENTY of wrong ways. If you say something positive, you will be hated for your patronizing tone. If you say something negative, you will be hated for your judgmentalism. If you say nothing, you will be hated for your indifference. Really, what is there to say? What words would make sense to a family who is sorting out the fact that their entire lives will be going down a very different sort of trajectory? There is nothing to take away the sting of the words, "your child is autistic." The pain has to be felt and worked through.

When you first get the diagnosis, it is so unfair, so wrong, that you have to be mad at someone. If you're going to direct your fury at something, though, it's good to be a bit pragmatic. It cannot be your child—it clearly isn't their fault. It would be great if it's not your spouse, though tensions between spouses often splinter a couple apart. But single parenting an autistic person is not easy, so it's good if your anger doesn't target the relationship with the one other person who loves your kid as much as you do. It makes sense to be angry with God, but God is a little too big, a little too abstract to absorb much direct heat. Plus, similar to the spouse, in the long run it's going to be good to keep a door open to a big potential source of solace and love. Making God the enemy could paint you into a corner down the road.

That's why the people who get the full extent of your wrath are going to most likely be bit players, or people who are symbolic of the injustice. One person in the medical team, a family support worker, a random stranger who says an inopportune something—these people and their one misplaced phrase will fester in you and finally give you a chance to vent out all of the emotion you've been hanging on to. God bless these safe people who may have no idea how horribly their words sat. During the grief process, someone has to be the villain. The anger needs to be directed somewhere.

So many parents I know hang on to one word or phrase that got their hackles up early on. A Family Services worker who thinks that what you really need is a bubble bath. A friend who says how lucky you are to have respite, a family member who suggests that maybe you ate too much junk food when you were pregnant. Years later, they can still tell the story of the one moment when they could feel the white-hot anger course through them. As the grief process continues, these moments can also lead to greater understanding of what we need to hear. My family doctor immediately wanted to put me on anti-depressants (and many moms legitimately need this route to keep both nostrils above water). What irked me was that it suggested that I needed to "buck up," that I needed to move past my grief and be strong. What I needed to hear was that my strength was not enough and did not need to be enough—we needed to make big changes in our family. I did not need to learn to cope with a husband who worked out of

18

town two weeks a month; I needed my husband to get a different job that allowed him to be more available. I didn't need an escape from reality—I needed a clear plan, therapeutic options and support to help my child learn and grow. I also really balked at any suggestion that I was weak or needy. Just a little quirk you learn when you grow up Mennonite. My mom's big expression growing up was "you're not sugar, you won't melt." Focusing on the reality that I WAS melting was terrifying and shameful for me. I needed to regain my dignity somehow, and that's why for me the focus on pragmatics helped me discover a sense of competence. Anything that focused on what I should be feeling was a real sore spot for me, and I've realized how much I have needed to give myself space to find my own voice and validate my own reactions. This has also helped me consider what Noah's experience is like, having no words and minimal control over his day. My reaction to people putting their own experience and expectations on me has taught me about how important it is for me to give Noah space to find his own sense of himself.

The flash of anger, then, sometimes leads to an insight about what you feel is important. Thinking about what it was that made you angry can become the turning point in finding words to help you move on.

But the anger can also move into a delicious stone of resentment you hide in your shoe, affecting every step as you limp along. Resentment can feel great, reinforcing how difficult your life is, how alone you are, how nobody understands. I am constantly having to shake the stones out of my shoes, still amazed at how easy it is to let them get in there, how secretly enjoyable it is to be the tortured victim.

3. Bargaining
David lived out this phase more clearly than I did and this isn't his book, but to quickly summarize—working really hard at your job and volunteering countless hours at church will:

a.Not convince God to heal your child of autism and
b.Not seem like a good idea to your spouse.

We've lived other forms of this stage throughout our journey. The special diets, the asking for prayer, the huge amounts of supplements and vitamins; they've all contributed to the idea that if we work hard enough, the autism will go away. Trying crazy therapies is not always a bad idea—my thinking about it now is that you need to try something if it's going to make you crazy with regret for not having tried it, but you also need to hold it loosely. It's not a hard bargain; it's just experimenting with what works and what doesn't.

When Noah was first diagnosed, David's mom mailed us a big batch of cookies, with a note to the effect of, "if life isn't sweet, you can at least eat a cookie." We embraced this logic with a vengeance for the first few years. If you can't get what you really want in life, take bites of facsimiles. This, of course, bit us in the ass. I had just quit my job of running a dance studio and teaching four hours a night, and the combination of cookies and no dancing resulted in 20 extra pounds. Feeling chubby really added to the sense that I was in control of my life (there's nothing like living out the change from vibrant leader/dancer/artist to overweight mother of disabled person to give you a special boost of "I can do it!") We also started smoking two cigarettes every Friday (this will be news to everyone in our family. When do you start hoping that your friends and family aren't actually reading your book?) There was a bit of defiance in this, certainly not an activity that was justifiable for people who were active in church and parenting young kids. My cousin was able to give me words to our logic at the time—we were playing with fire, sending out smoke signals to the universe; something is wrong! Please send help!

These are not classic descriptions of the "bargaining" stage of grief (and in case you haven't noticed, I'm not presenting an academic paper, here). But for me, it felt like a bargain, specifically with God. Or maybe the back end of a previously unspoken bargain: we'll be good people who do good things; you'll give us a good life. If you're going to make it hard, then we're not going to be responsible.

Of course, it was a bad bargain. The sugar, the smoking, the extra glass of wine, none of those small pleasures got us any closer to realizing our hopes for our family or for ourselves. We've moved through that phase, and we don't need those vices anymore (though we do maintain a soft spot for dark chocolate on bad days). It didn't really help, and now I'm at a deficit in terms of body image and energy levels. The 20 pounds turned into thirty, which is exactly how much I gained for each pregnancy. So I've been carrying my own little "grief baby" for the last while. Maybe it's time for delivery. In the meantime, at least there is Spanx ®.

4. Depression
Ah. Depression. What can I say? It sucks. It is dark and grey and heavy. You remember that you are made for sunshine, but you can't find your way out. It will pass.

There is so much talk about depression that it has lost all meaning. There is a difference between the dark night that your soul requires to make the adjustment from one kind of life to another, and the clinical diagnosis. The former is difficult and dark, but it can lead to a deeper sense of what it means to be alive and a sense of the very real meaning behind a lot of potentially cheesy Hallmark sayings. It's a personal and intimate time. If you ignore this time, or if you stay in it too long, it can become the latter—a reshaping of how your brain functions. Just remember the basic care for any life form. Feed and water yourself daily. Find a sunny patch. You will begin to see in colour again.

5. Adjustment
Here's a stage that I just flat out made up. I've noticed that most of the moms I know have gone through a physical stage of adjustment as part of their grief work. When your

child is first diagnosed, you go into a kind of sprint, learning about therapy models, advocating for your child, researching interventions. You're busy girding up the foundations of your child's life and learning approaches. Then, when your child is about age ten, your body calls a time out. There needs to be a shift from sprint to marathon. My year was the spring after Noah's accident. We went from the accident, to a big fundraiser for his service dog, and then a family tragedy (the death of my step-sister). About a month after that, I got an infection that required surgery. For months after, I parented from the couch, unable to get my energy back. Word is, it had something to do with the fact that my adrenal glands had entirely pooped out. A friend of mine had mono for a year. Another got strep. Our bodies took whatever excuse they could to take a well-deserved time out. If you are a parent of an autistic child who is under the age of ten.....erm. Sorry. Don't let it get you down. Just accept that sometimes your body will fail you and if you let it rest, it will get a chance to reset to marathon pace. (Though, as per my grief-baby belly, carb loading will not be your friend, here.) Medicating your way through this phase will not make it go away any faster, but it might be the only way to get through.

6. Acceptance

A weird thing about autism is that it is nebulous—everyone has heard a miracle story, I know of children who have officially lost their diagnosis. I don't know if this stage would be easier if Noah had, say, Down's Syndrome, or his legs were amputated or something. Would it be easier if I was dealing with a diagnosis from which there wasn't hope for a "cure?" Part of my advocacy work for ABA (Applied Behaviour Analysis) therapy is convincing the government that some children with the diagnosis lose it through consistent ABA. The fact that I've been running an ABA program for the last 12 years, and that it's been good quality and fairly consistent, has not changed the fact that my boy is still profoundly autistic. At a certain point, though, I stopped running a program to take away Noah's autism and started to think of it as building in skills that he will need to cope with his diagnosis better (and also building skills that will help the rest of us cope with him better.)

An acquaintance was telling me of a family who was "strong in prayer," whose son just started talking when he turned 18. And talking completely casually and fluently. Overnight, his diagnosis was gone. This always happens to acquaintances that heard about it. I have never met a kid like this, though I have heard of verifiable accounts of a child who has learned to cope with their diagnosis so well that they are indistinguishable from their peers. I think that's pretty different. I thought about what that would be like. Noah comes downstairs one morning and says, "Hey Mom, what's for breakfast? I think I'll walk to school myself today." Part of my mind exploded at the longing for that kind of interaction, the ease of language. But part of me also thought about the bunny I live with now, so bouncy and happy and weird. I would really miss him. Oh the irony. Part of the thrill of a miracle would demand some grief work for the autistic boy that I knew and loved.

The change has happened over time, and certainly there are moments when I have to grieve deeper layers of all of this. When all of my friends' kids are old enough not to need a babysitter and I see them getting a fresh lease on life and enjoying the independence. When my niece and nephew surpass their older cousin within the first year and a half of life. When my older son graduates from school and moves into a big world full of possibilities, and adventures and independence.

THINGS THAT ARE WRONG WITH ME

When Noah was first diagnosed, a lot of people had helpful comments to make sense of the whole thing. I was such a saint, God was probably blessing me. I had sinned in some way and God was probably punishing me. Either way, it seemed that autism and me were meant to be.

None of those philosophies ring true to me. I'm inadequate enough to be disqualified from any saint standing, but not really mean-hearted enough to get singled-out for my level of sin. I'm basically lazy and naive—especially when I was starting to have kids. I imagined myself as a pretty zen mom. Someone you could talk to about anything. Dysfunctional enough to make life interesting, but loving enough to give my kids a sense of stability. David and I had planned to both work part-time so that we could both enjoy jobs without having to give up the fun of hanging out with the kids. I'm an artist and performer and imagined a bohemian life, with lots of crazy memory-making times and minimal housework. I remember when my mom came to help and suggested that I do a load of laundry every day. I preferred the drama of having absolutely nothing to wear and then going to the laundromat and eating take-out chicken balls while we commandeered seven washing machines at a time. I love being just on the edge of chaos.

When we get a rainstorm, the first thing I want to do is run in the ravine in front of our house, getting soaked and feeling wild.

None of these characteristics are helpful for raising a child with autism.

Autistic people usually do well with structure, a fairly rigid schedule and stability. I hardly know the meaning of those words. If you want flights of fancy, I'm your gal, but if you want steady follow through, well.... that's my kryptonite.

So, yes, I get the whole "edge of chaos" being a good match for living with an autistic person, but is there anything about me that could be helpful for Noah? If God "chose" to give Noah to me, what was the exact rationale?

Believe me, I majored in psychology and developmental studies in my undergrad. I studied autism. I found it UNINTERESTING.

For the first year after Noah's diagnosis, I was overwhelmed with options and emotions. Then I did what any normal mother of a child who needs early intervention did—I produced a CD to express my feelings about it. I don't have any discernible musical talent, but music means a lot to me. And I do have a lot of talented friends. I put together a CD of songs that my friends donated to articulate the story of hope, grief, love and mystery that I was going through. We used the sales from that CD to raise money for a therapy program for Noah. And I also used it to wrangle three more credits for my graduate degree. It was the only thing I could do—before I could move into action, I had to create something that would help me find words to express my feelings about it.

The "right" mother for Noah would have done a bit more research on autism. Maybe she would have dug right into ABA; the therapy program that we chose when he was three and have been using since. She would have a visual schedule for activities THAT SHE WOULD BE ABLE TO MAINTAIN. She would have a practical mindset and probably be happy and capable whipping up batches of gluten-free muffins. Surely she would be able to remember if it was Day 1 or Day 2 at school (and what that meant).

I am someone who can get so engrossed in a book that I forget about reality. If I'm in the middle of reading, I don't hear other people talking to me; when I start a book, I can't stop until it's done, even if it means staying up until 3am. Sometimes I forget about reality with no book as an excuse. I spent all of the boys' years in elementary school using the oven timer to remind me to pick them up at lunch and again after school. Time being fluid is great if you're a mystic, but not so helpful if you're up against the needs of an institution that expects mothers to be time-sensitive, detail-oriented and ready to spring into action with a dozen cookies for the bake sale at a moment's notice.

So, not only am I a right-brained, creative type striving for relevance and marketability in the "real" world ("following my bliss" has resulted in an MA in theology with an emphasis on embodied spirituality—not exactly a career path teeming with job opportunities and financial security), I am also an ADHD, emotional mom striving for relevance in the world of autism. If my kids were neurotypical, they could cover for some of my weaknesses. But Noah isn't helped by my weakness. He needs persistence and order. He needs someone who doesn't get overwhelmed by the task of assembling one hundred different pieces of stimulus for a sorting program, or prepping 50 different sentence combinations with photos for the iPad (I will EASILY suggest these programs and start collecting stuff. But halfway through, it becomes so daunting and so seemingly endless that I begin to struggle. It doesn't help that I know there will be 50 more things to prep the following week. The need for novel material is never satiated.)

I have slowly learned that I need outside supports to help me figure all of this out.

Because of Noah's atypical presentation, I'm pretty sure he's got a double helping of brain wiring issues. Once doctors diagnose autism, they stop looking for other conditions, but I'm sure that Noah is also ADHD. Some of the writing about ADHD has helped me understand what Noah needs. It has completely helped me understand what I need. I am the person stealthily reading the ADHD self-help books in the bookstore, getting ideas about how to find order. Nothing about order has come naturally to me, I have had to learn coping strategies to keep our house going.

This is one of the major reasons I chose ABA. It is the complete opposite of me—rigorous, thorough, objective, analytical. It breaks everything down into manageable chunks and teaches one skill at a time, building slowly towards success. It is humbling and counterintuitive for me. But it does create a structure for both me and Noah to follow.

In reading about my weaknesses, you may now judge me as unintelligent or incapable. Unfit to mother. This is certainly how I judge myself much of the time. Maybe it's because I am coming out of a fairly conservative, evangelical background, where all women were assumed to have innate household skills and interests. Maybe it's because I have so many friends who are very granola—cooking all of their food from scratch, investing whole-heartedly into making every single decision a child-centred, eco-friendly one. I can't measure up. I can't help that my gifts are in creating things, appreciating beauty and other non-essential skills.

The super-parenting that I see around me shames me. All of the skills that come naturally to these other moms feel like rocket science to me. The judgment I have for myself is paralyzing. I am shamed by the heartfelt YouTube videos of smiling moms who say that they love their disabled kids and never needed to grieve, because they love their kids unconditionally. God saw them through. Everything is great.

Well, I needed to grieve. I needed to grieve long and hard. Now I wonder why. Noah has had such a good year. I'm starting to forget how hard it was when he was hell-bent on getting himself killed. He is so happy and lovely now; I forget how scared I was initially at the thought of a non-verbal teenager who was bigger than me, a 40-year-old who would still be living with me and needing help in the shower. And his life is full of experiences now, but all I could think of back then were all the experiences he wouldn't have—getting married, being independent, reminiscing with me.

Focusing on my inadequacies hasn't helped me be a better mother. I eventually had to admit defeat in some areas and learn how to have compassion for myself. Everyone else seems to be better at figuring all of this out (I probably look like I have it figured out to everyone else too.) It is humbling to have to learn some basic organizational skills because they do not come naturally to me. Or to accept that some things that have been insurmountable obstacles in my life are tiny little hurdles in someone else's. What I need is self-compassion. And I would love to be in a place where some of my strengths might get a little attention too. I couldn't have survived parenting without finding places to play, to create, to dance; to do the things that highlight what I do bring to the world, not just focus on the things I lack.

Noah looks at my life and probably sees it as rocket science too. I ask him what he did at school and he tells me what school he attends. "Yes, but what did you DO?" I ask. "At school" he answers. Exactly. This conversational gag goes on day after day. Increasingly, he is able to hang on long enough to dredge up a word or two to describe his day. "Swimming." "Movie." And I check his notebook to confirm he really did go swimming, or if a movie was part of the day. It is so hard for me to remember to do this every day after school, for consistency. It is so hard for him to go through all of the elements of what I'm asking—memory, labeling, attending to another person. But we do it. Because focusing on how inadequate this conversation is won't help us. We need to keep learning.

Then I make him hug me, because we both need it, even though only one of us seems to be interested. Then we make a snack and colour because it's also good to celebrate the fun things. And Noah probably thinks it's a good thing that I'm fresh out of gluten-free organic muffins anyway.

SOMEBODY FARTED

Maybe I have difficulties with polite conversation. Or maybe I'm socially deficient. But I just don't seem to be able to master small talk. It's especially hard when I'm meeting new people, treading water in a sea of easy chatter. All of the stories I've got aren't really icebreakers, they're anvils. It might start easily enough. If people are telling stories about their kids, I pause before adding one of my own. No, I think, this one is innocent enough, and then I say something, perhaps about Baby Tiger and how he has travelled everywhere with us. Someone will try to continue the conversation and innocently ask how old my son is. "Fifteen" I will say, realizing that there might be a bit of a back-story missing about why my teenager still cares about Baby Tiger. It's not that I'm ashamed of Noah's diagnosis, or that I'm trying to pass as "normal" (I don't need autism to out me as odd). It's just that it's going to take a moment for the other person to recover, to inject a little autism anecdote of their own or offer a word of pity, and by then the rhythm of the conversation has missed a step and we flounder on, coming to surface jokes and safe exchanges. The weight of my story threatens to strain the easygoing patter of new meetings. It's a moment of intimacy; a glimpse of an alternate life and it comes unexpectedly.

Am I overly sensitive? Do I expect a pity reaction and that's why "the reveal" is so difficult? Or is it that my life is so different from yours that as soon as I say anything, it will become obvious that we are going to have to shout at each other over a chasm of assumptions and expectations? Because, when I hear you go on about how funny your child is, or how smart, or how busy you are driving your kid to lessons, I have to translate in my head. How can I share a funny story about my bunny without having to explain Noah's rule of Words-That-Shall-Not-Be-Named? How do I brag about my child's accomplishments when they involve showering by himself, beginning to read and not requiring a call to 911 for several months? How do I sympathize with your busy schedule when I would happily trade my schedule of respite workers, funding reports and therapy with yours?

Once people know me and have heard my story, it's fine. We get used to speaking from different planets and I truly can empathize with you because your kid is talking back to you. I get that there are different levels of "hard" when it comes to parenting and I understand that it is actually sometimes harder to deal with a kid who CAN talk, but refuses to.

My life is not bad, but it's different. The moments between "Nice to meet you" and "Tell me about yourself" are golden, when we can happily assume that we have something in common, some frame of reference that is shared. I know there's an elephant in the room, and I'm fine letting you know too, but I really hope the elephant doesn't shock you, or choose that particular moment to trumpet loudly.

If I'm at a baby shower, I'm especially aware of my elephant. We pass the baby around, commenting on how perfect he is, how adorable. The mother is nervous and I confidently tell her that there's nothing to worry about, that everything will be fine. In the silence that follows, as recollections of my story filter through different people at the shower, especially that mother who voiced her concern to me specifically because I represent everything that she fears about mothering, my elephant farts noisily, leaving a stench in the room. It clouds everything. The reality sinks in. My baby was passed around like this too, and nobody had any idea that he was wired differently. Nobody would have guessed that one day he'd be in a wheelchair, or almost drowned, or that he'd burn down the house, only to try again two years later.

The air clears out and the conversation turns back to easy, light conversations. But I look at that new mom and I can tell her with absolute sincerity, "Everything really will be fine." The elephant nods in agreement.

THE OTHER SON

I have another son.

Born 19 months before Noah, Jase was our sunshine. He was an imaginative, energetic, charismatic little guy. At a family gathering when Jase was two, he climbed on top of a coffee table and happily directed all of his great-aunts and uncles in a sing-a-long. He endeared himself to our elderly neighbours, going over for visits to eat soup and play chess, running through their sprinkler with an umbrella to cover his head. He was King of the Mountain.

When he was in preschool, an exercise required us to use three words to describe our kids. Jase was: sensitive, intense and delightful. As sunny as his usual disposition was, his intensity could sometimes get the best of him. My mom compared him to the girl with a curl on her forehead—when she was good, she was very, very good, but when she was bad, she was horrid. When Jase was good, he was magical. Inquisitive, passionate and commanding. But when his sensitivity overtook his ability to communicate, he would have a tantrum and shout. Our church at the time had a communication system with the children's program downstairs, and I remember many times when Jase's number would pop up and I'd have to run interference. If his sense of justice was threatened, he would yell and hit, sometimes banging his head against the wall. We called him Volcano Boy.

If Jase was the sun, then Noah was the moon: round and passive, mysterious and quiet. He was so much easier to parent than Jase. So much less volatile. When it was time to make a decision about our next child (we had always imagined we'd have three or four), it was Jase's needs that made us reconsider. Our fear was that, between the demands of a newborn and Jase's volatility, our middle child, Noah, would disappear completely. We were already having a hard time connecting with him. Later, of course, it was the ongoing question; when Noah bolts, would I let him run or would I drop the baby to go after him? that would ultimately solidify our decision not to have any more kids.

We had purposely had our children close together, in an effort to make sure that they would be friends through life. Our thinking was that if Jase didn't fully remember being an only child, then we would conveniently skip all of the bad feelings of giving up that coveted spot that toddlers go through. This was a fail on so many levels.

Jase went through the classic, "I hate this new thing that's taking all the attention" phase with a vengeance. Noah threatened his universe and he let us know that the infiltrator was not appreciated. One of the first things Noah did when he learned how to walk was how to hunker into a safety stance when Jase came in the room. He was very used to getting knocked over.

This is classic behaviour, but it usually gets resolved once the baby turns into a toddler and becomes an ally of the older child. However, for my dear Jase, when the baby turned into a toddler and received a diagnosis, it became clear that the sun was going to be eclipsed by the moon forever.

I don't know what happens in the mind of a toddler when the little brother you've always pushed away is suddenly pronounced "broken." When you see your mom lying on the floor crying while your little brother runs circles around her for hours. When it finally dawns on you that your grabs for attention are falling on deaf ears. Do you wonder if you caused it? Do you blame yourself? My poor sunshine boy. You who already are so sensitive and so intense, there will not be words to describe the strong emotions that you are feeling. The confidence you had in being King of the Mountain has been shattered, and your parents have become strangers.

Eventually, things improved. Jase went to school and had some distance from Noah. He was in a class that had a lot of structure, which suited him really well (and was a new experience for him. Structure's not my strong suit and two parents who are self-employed don't have any semblance of routine.) He found friends. He found Lego. Later on, he found poetry and music, his dearest companions.

Over the years, I think we've been able to get at some of the questions. I've explained autism and hopefully have stated strongly enough that he is not to blame for it. Jase once commented that it was clear that Noah didn't like him and I hope I've been able to convey the reality that Noah seems like he's rejecting, but it's not personal. Anytime that Jase has opened up, I have tried to meet his emotions with reassurance. But how much is left unopened? I have no idea.

Jase is now a model teenager. He is socially conscious, bright, thoughtful and diligent. He won the top award for marks in his grade last year, as well as the citizenship award. He practices guitar, banjo and piano for hours every day and says foreign things like, "I'm feeling full, so I won't have dessert." His orthodontist had to make a special note on his file, because he actually wore his elastics and followed all the rules scrupulously, so his teeth fell into line a little too quickly. His room is the cleanest in the house.

He has a list of stores that he refuses to shop from on moral grounds and prefers hemp t-shirts.

This might sound like he's a bore, but he's also a really cool guy. He collects vinyl and has a thing for bluegrass. He supports indie bands and writes poetry and songs, paints and makes really interesting art. Seriously. He's a kid you want to know.

I asked him once if he remembered Volcano Boy and Jase said, "He's still here, I've just learned to have him explode on the inside." Erm..... great. So, we're saving up for therapy bills in his future.

I have talked to a few siblings of special-needs kids, and an ongoing theme is that they see their parents working hard to handle things and decide that they will help by not having personal needs of their own. Jase's favourite phrases are, "I'm sorry" and "Don't worry about me."

We go back and forth on how to handle parenting Jase. In many ways, we're parenting two only children. Except that Jase gets none of the attention and opportunities that an only child would get. We feel badly for him; his entire experience of the world is flavoured by autism, whereas David and I at least have a "pre" experience to draw from, in terms of defining what is normal, what it's like to live with less stress. Jase lives with scrutiny from others ('fess up, did you wonder if Jase was on the spectrum when I mentioned that he banged his head? People do it all the time. They like a biological link. Jase has been congratulated on his eye contact more than most kids.)

I see the many ways that Noah has shaped Jase's personality. I don't know if it's intentional or not, but Jase has turned out to be the perfect foil for Noah. Noah attracts attention, Jase prefers to be invisible. Noah is impulsive, Jase is doggedly diligent. Noah is a little too open with his body, Jase is intensely private. Noah has a huge carbon footprint, Jase recycles fastidiously. Noah loves pop music and culture, Jase likes vintage culture—folk music. Noah is my toddler forever. Jase is already an old man.

We draw a lot of attention, what with the purple dog, the police escorts, the general hopping and flapping that surrounds us. For an introverted teenager, Jase doesn't appreciate being part of the spectacle. He doesn't invite friends to our house because either Noah makes them uncomfortable or Jase is nervous that there will be inadvertent nudity or shouting. Even though he's been steeped in our version of normal, he's painfully aware that other people don't live like us. Between an odd brother and crazy parents who have lost all sense of normal, and tend to break into song and find themselves hilarious, Jase stays in his own room or goes to his friends' houses to hang out.

We have tried to make it up to Jase in many ways. Reading is a main way that our family bonds and we have spent hours reading through long sagas. Even now, as a teenager, he still lets me read to him, especially during the summer. I will read while Jase and David watch Noah in the lake and we can go for ten hours if tea keeps being delivered. I relish the chance to share my love of reading; the escape to different worlds, with at least one of my kids. It would seem that my work with Jase is to call him out to new lands, whereas my work with Noah is to call him into reality.

When Jase was in grade seven, I decided to try homeschooling since we were going to do some travelling that year anyway. It was so great to be at home with Jase without Noah around. It felt like a righting of the balance to focus my energy and teaching on him. We ended up having so much fun that we decided to try it for another year before Jase started worrying that I wasn't working him as hard as his friends at school and that he might be falling behind. We have tried to make sure that Jase doesn't constantly get the short end of the stick in terms of time and energy. Sometimes Jase suggests that we might be trying too hard and will encourage me to stop psychologizing him and talking about our feelings all the time so he can practice guitar.

We have also been aware of building people into Jase's life. Noah has a team of people who work with him all the time, and those people grow to love him. I am so grateful for the team, yet I'm aware that Jase doesn't have an accompanying entourage to support and encourage him. My chosen sister, Catherine, has always had a special love for Jase and we've occasionally flown him out to Vancouver to see her for a week and let him be the sole recipient of her attention. His closest friend's family has also adopted him in a way. After the fire, we just sent Jase to their house for two weeks, knowing that he'd be protected from the worst of the smoke and stress. It's a hard choice sometimes, to give him up. I wish that I could be that refuge for him, but often it is an act of love to allow him to be embraced by others too.

During Noah's bolting days, Jase was constantly parenting Noah, and he was a much bossier parent than David or me. We tried to protect him from the stress of worrying about Noah, telling him to back off and keeping him uninvolved even though Jase could see David and I take turns keeping watch with military precision. When we used to go camping, we didn't want Jase to feel responsible if Noah woke up in the middle of the night and left the camper, so I would sleep with Noah and David would sleep with Jase instead of throwing the boys together. In the morning, it was David, not me, who had a difficult sleep—we hadn't realized that Jase woke up several times a night, sitting up and asking, "Where's Noah?" Jase was just as worried as we were. When we told him not to worry, he challenged us and told us that he also loved Noah and why wouldn't he be worried? It's been an ongoing challenge to acknowledge that Jase needs to be involved in the security issues, but that his involvement needs to be manageable.

Lately, I've been moving into another style of parenting, focusing on resilience. Realistically, there's a whole lot of things we DO provide Jase: two parents who are happily married, a lot of love, and just enough crazy to keep life interesting. We have all had to forgive Noah at some level for being autistic. He's not going to be the little brother who looks up to his big brother like a hero. He might destroy your things (Jase does at least have a lock on his door to prevent that from happening too often.) He might not be the companion you were hoping for. But he is your brother.

A few key things have happened lately to start shifting our family dynamic. First, there is a realization that not all brothers get along. Even without the autism, Noah would be sporty, flirty, goofy and into pop music. He might not appreciate Jase's hipster vibe even if he did have social skills. They would still fight over the evil of McDonald's (one solidly for, one dead against). It's not like autism is the only thing that differentiates these two.

Second, I've stopped apologizing for the family we have. I love these boys. I wouldn't trade either of them. It doesn't help to wish that things were different. There's a big "get over it" that our family is clambering over, tortoise-like.

This is not resolved. I am crying as I write this, because I never meant for either of my kids to have such a hard road. But I know that hardship has contributed to both of their characters, and their characters are both so delightful. I wish sometimes that we had had that third baby, that Jase would have an ally in this crazy world, especially as we get older. That there would be someone else that he could laugh at all of this with. But there isn't anyone else. I will have to trust that what we have is enough and that Jase's experience of family will extend beyond blood.

MAKING UP IS HARD TO DO

Pets always seem like a good idea. We got a cat from the Humane Society when the boys were about three and five. Noah didn't register any kind of interest in this new creature for the first eight months, and then, out of nowhere, fell suddenly and deeply in love with it. So in love that, after about a year of zealous loving, we realized the cat was going to either lose his winning personality or his ability to survive excessive cuddling by an ever-stronger admirer. The cat needed an early retirement, and we found a family that lived outside of town who were more than happy to gently love our kitty. It was a heart-breaker for our whole family, especially Jase. But it had been the right thing to do for a number of reasons—excessive squishing aside, our older boy had dark rings around his eyes and a nose that was always stuffed. A few months after the cat left, the "cold" that had been dogging Jase for the last two years abated.

Jase was broken-hearted about the cat. No amount of talking about allergies would help, but there was a simmering feeling of injustice over the feeling that Noah's zealousness cost Jase his most beloved buddy. When you are parenting a special needs child, and you know FULL WELL that your time and attention are not being divided evenly, you can lose perspective. We wanted to do something for Jase that would meet his need for a companion without sacrificing his sinuses. We didn't want him to lose one more experience of childhood because of his brother. I suggested a snake, since Jase had been interested in them for some time. David and Jase returned from the pet store with a breeding pair, because it's not enough to have one snake when you can have a home-based snake breeding business that will teach entrepreneurial skills as well as providing the love and attention of a typical reptile. If one snake was going to be Good for Jase, then two would be Good Enough to Make Up For the Time Noah Ate Your Goldfish and Other Events (non-specified, to protect the innocent by reason of autism).

For the next year and a half, we bred around 70 snakes, experienced two major escapes (including one 22-baby-snake-break-out), bought dozens of frozen mice for meals and over-saturated the Winnipeg market with corn snakes, thereby reducing the value of the breed. I think I was actually up for Mother of the Year during the first part of our run—if anything will convince a jury of peers of your dedication to your child, there's nothing like showing up to school with a pregnant snake wrapped around your neck for show and tell. Alas, word of the escapes spread through the neighbourhood and friends refused to set foot in the house for years after. Our time with snakes is, perhaps, a different book (or maybe a survival manual), but what we learned by the end of it was:

1. No amount of snake is going to make up for a fluffy friend who will purr on your lap.
2. Three hours of teaching a baby snake to consume a baby mouse may not be considered "quality" time with your child.
3. The injustice of living with a high-needs brother is not going to be overcome with reptiles.

THE ACCIDENT

It was a dark and stormy night. Noah was having a sleepover at Mom's house and David and I were in our makeshift gazebo, having a drink and enjoying the storm from our protected vantage point. The rain was making it cold, so David went in to get a blanket. When he went in the house, the phone was ringing and he picked it up. All he could hear was, "Noah's missing" before it went dead.

This is not the first time that we had gotten that call. Noah had gone missing on us, a few respite workers, and Mom—many times before. But not in the middle of the night. I could hear sirens on Osborne— the main street half a block away. There are always sirens in a lightning storm, but it added to the tension of the moment. Everything felt electric. I grabbed my cell phone and went to the car. If it was our house, I'd know which direction to head out in, but I didn't know where Noah would go from Mom's. She's near a train track, the legislative building, the Forks—all places that interest Noah. David stayed behind a moment to gather flashlights and headlamps. He imagined a long night in the dark trying to find and follow Noah's path. We hatched a quick plan; I'd drive to Mom's and start searching until he could meet us in the second car.

I drove down Osborne while sobbing to the 911 operator. "He's a little boy. He's eight. He's autistic. He can't talk!" It's maybe a three-minute drive to Mom's, but it felt endless. Until I got closer and realized that police had shut Osborne down. Police tape cordoned off the road and emergency lights were flashing everywhere. He wasn't lost, I realized with a jolt. "There's been an accident," I shouted. "He's been hit." I ran from our car over to the police officer, who got me off the phone and tried to calm me.

Apparently Mom had been in her duplex and had noticed that the sirens were not continuing down the road. Something had happened right near her house. With a sinking feeling, she went to check on Noah, who had been fast asleep. All she could see now was an empty bed and the curtain blowing in the wind.

We think he had woken up with the lightning and then been dazzled by the "Robin's Donuts" sign across the road. He climbed out of the window, onto the garden shed and across Osborne before an SUV intersected his path.

Mom called us while running down the back lane, at which point her phone lost its signal and went dead. When she got to the accident site, the ambulance was already gone. We found each other quickly, both lost in our own sense of panic and shame. I had only had one drink, but the smell of alcohol on my breath and my crying, bewildered state must have made me look like I was a parenting course drop-out. My mom felt responsible, but my only thought was "I should have been there." The mother arriving late to the scene, unable to speak coherently. Unable to be trusted to raise this elusive boy. "Where were you?" the police officer's question tore through my brain, shredding my resolve.

David came soon after, quickly assessing that we didn't need a search party, we needed to get to the hospital. Jase was still asleep at Mom's, so she stayed behind. I left my car on Osborne, and am still not sure who ended up moving it or when it was returned to my house. We joined the traffic jam that had been caused by the road closure and slowly wound our way through the alleys to get back on to the main street. I was dimly aware that they needed to keep the road closed to do their measurements. If Noah died, there would be an investigation. Nobody had heard yet what the outcome was, though we did know that he was alive when they took him away.

As we crawled through an alley, a man approached the car with a notebook. "Do you know what happened?" And I, the measure of grace under pressure, started babbling and crying about my baby. When we are vulnerable like this, David knows to withdraw and focus. I fall apart and desperately need to connect, to process the unbelievable through a steady stream of verbal diarrhea. I don't know why the reporter came to our car. I don't know if he judged me in that moment. Or if he understood that Noah was loved and attended to constantly, that there was a diagnosis involved, that I normally do cope under everyday pressure. But I felt completely naked. He saw the part of me that I desperately try to protect. I was living out my worst nightmare and I could not cope.

As we drove to the hospital, I collapsed. Sobbing and wailing. It was almost an out-of- body experience. And David drove on, rock solid and focused on getting there. He finally said I had to pull myself together. It was not going to help Noah if I was having histrionics. I knew this too. I also knew that I wouldn't get a chance to process these emotions once I got to emergency. I would need to be strong for Noah and then later for Jase. I would need to comfort Mom, who would be feeling terrible. This was my only chance to purge myself of all of this panic and fear, to let my guard down, and I had no responsibility in that moment, except to make space for these emotions. This is a difference between us. I am a fall-apart-and-pull-myself-together kind of person. I'm not sure if David has ever fallen apart fully yet. We have our own rhythm of coping, I guess. We never would have made it to the hospital if we had both given in to the pain.

I gave myself five minutes while driving and then started reigning in the snot and tears. When we got to the hospital, we were ushered immediately into the trauma room. After several other experiences of waiting for hours in emergency with babies, trying to convince medical staff that something was wrong, this time we were rushed through, no questions asked. Once we had this experience, I never again bemoaned having to wait—waiting means that they assume you'll live. It's a good thing.

Noah was strapped to a board and panicking, unable to look around. I stood where he could see me and put my hand on his chest. It was deeply comforting to me to see him recognize me, to meet the fear in his eyes with the assurance that he would be ok. His eyes locked on mine and his body stopped trembling. In the middle of the panic over this whole situation, I did not take for granted that my presence would matter to him. It was a gift to realize that he did know us, did care about us, even though he hadn't expressed that through eye contact or social situations before.

Then it was a matter of going over his body and reading the story of pain it was telling. The fender of the car hit his femur, breaking it. As he folded in half from the impact, his head hit the front of the car, fracturing his skull. The driver had been braking as soon as she caught sight of him, but the momentum was too much. Once he was hit, the SUV ran over him, leaving tire tracks on his stomach and splitting his liver. As it finally came to a stop, it dragged his body along the pavement, taking the skin off his wrist right down to the bone and leaving black lines of asphalt in his hip that still mark him today, years later.

As they worked over him, cleaning and stitching, they realized that a vein had been crushed and he would be in danger of amputation if they gave him a typical cast. He went in to surgery to get an external fixator—basically installing four screws into his femur, which were connected by an external metal pole that fixed the bone in place.

During this time David had gone to Mom's, knowing that she would want to be in the hospital and see Noah. We all needed to see that he was alive, to touch him and hold on to him. David also wanted to be the one who would be at her house when Jase woke up, to be the one to tell the story of what happened. Over the next four days, we took turns at the hospital, learned how to care for his wounds and got used to the wheelchair that Noah would need for the next three months. David built a ramp to the house and we got a hospital bed for the living room. During this time, a friend took a shift at the hospital so that we could take Jase out for his birthday supper. We headed to the Olive Garden, a group of the walking wounded filling up on pasta and salad in celebration of this other son, who could think of nothing more exciting than never-ending bowls of Greek salad just one week before.

Our church and friends rallied in a way they never had before. Suppers were dropped off, people were genuinely concerned and there for us. I was grateful, but aware that my experience once again did not match the perception of those around me. Although it was a stressful, demanding time, it was also a miracle. We had lived through my worst nightmare. And we continued living. There was no funeral to plan, no goodbyes to make. My boy recognized me, and my presence mattered to him. And, not to be flippant, a boy in a wheelchair was a chance to rest. About three weeks after the accident, Noah tried escaping again. But when your escape plan involves scooching out the door on your butt, traveling inches an hour, it's just pathetic, not fear-inducing.

He had lived. He knew us. And he was not going anywhere for three months. It was a good summer.

A DOG AND HIS BOY

First there is the hoping.

You hear about a service dog who will, "enrich the quality of life and enhance the independence of children and families living with autism" (National Service Dogs website). You think about Lassie saving Timmy from the well. You think maybe an extra set of eyes and furry companionship might be the ticket to safety.

It took a few years of waffling to sign up for a service dog. After trying the nutritional supplements, the crazy diets, the balance boards, I thought it would be worth considering. On cold wintry nights, when we were sacked-out in front of the TV, David would turn to me and say, "Who'd be walking the dog today?" and I'd realize that a dog would be too much work for us. We were overwhelmed with life as it was. We couldn't imagine adding anything else to the mix.

Then Noah went through a wave of escapes one year that left me crippled with anxiety. It started early spring, when Noah ran across the river while it was melting. My mom went running after him and we almost lost them both. After we retrieved them, we had to pick up the toboggan my mom had been pulling Noah on, and we saw huge puddles in each footstep heading across the river. About a month later, Noah escaped and all David could find was his pile of wet clothes at the riverbank. (He had ditched the clothes after realizing the water was cold and proceeded over the bridge in his underwear to get to a yellow plastic slide he had spotted across the water.) I had been on the phone with 911, so I knew Noah had been found and was being delivered back to us, but David was by the edge of the water for a while, looking for a little blonde head to come popping up from the water.

There were so many times that spring when the community got involved in looking for Noah that, when I decided to take up jogging, two neighbours and a passing motorist each called out on different occasions to see if I needed help. They've all learned to differentiate my "panic" face from my "chubby lady running" face (completely different shades of red.) We finally realized that the safety a dog might provide would more than pay for the extra responsibilities we'd have to take-on, so we completed the forms, enclosed a deposit, and mailed the application off to the closest program, in Ontario.

Then there is the waiting.

Once we realized how long the wait would be, we wished we had just thrown that piece of paper into the mail when we first heard about it. We could have had three years to waffle to our hearts' content. But we didn't. We asked for a dog at our breaking point, when we felt that the chance of Noah surviving the year was negligible. It felt like the only way the cycle was going to end was at his funeral.

That August was the summer that landed Noah in a wheelchair. In that whole hullaballoo, the reset button was finally found. Noah began to trust us, to learn to be the tiniest bit afraid of running. Jase stopped waking up in the middle of the night yelling, "Where's Noah?" We unclenched ever so slightly. And we kept waiting for the dog.

And then the begging...

Although service dogs are technically free to any child with autism, it costs $24,000 to raise one (or it did at the time. It's up to $30,000 now). You don't "buy" a service dog; you receive it free with a strong encouragement to raise the money so the program will continue. It does make sense, though. People connect with a particular child and want to support that child—it's easier for the program to be sustainable if everyone getting a dog pitches in. Seeing as how we didn't have an extra $24,000 lying around, we needed to raise money. When we were running a private ABA program with Noah (costing $30,000/year because we had to fly a consultant in from Wisconsin and pay all of our workers), we had raised some money. But once the program became government-funded people didn't know how to help. This dog was a concrete way of supporting us, and our community rallied. Two women helped me organize a fantastic social, get on Shaw TV to tell people about our cause, and partner with Petland to support Noah. Complete strangers heard about our story on CBC radio and supported us. People just love the idea of a dog and a boy.

The money was raised pretty quickly. People were eager to help. The hard part was asking in the first place. The act of admitting to the public that I could not handle my son on my own and needed help was the first step in what I initially would call, "my breakdown" and would later term, "getting over myself." An ongoing battle...

The best part of this time was at the "social"—a gathering specific to Manitobans. People usually do it to raise money for an upcoming wedding, but it can be for any "cause." I had been so involved in planning and feeling badly about asking for help that I had forgotten the point of the thing in the first place. In the middle of it, I realized that 400 people had bought tickets and come out to support my son. They fundamentally wanted him to be safe and alive. For all of the petty anger I have carried over the years about people not saying exactly the right thing upon diagnosis, or not being there in the everyday support of our family, I realized that the general attitude toward Noah is one of care and concern. People are not against him, or concerned about the fact that he is demanding and different. But they are often ignorant about how to help. That's very different than being unwilling to help. This is an example of when another step of courage is required on my part to, first of all, know what we need, and how to ask for it. It was also a turning point for our family. We realized that some people were there because of Noah, not because they were friends of Noah's parents. And some people were there because of Jase. Our boys were becoming their own people, with their own communities and friendship groups. It was a shift and an encouragement to me. People are drawn to my kids because they are interesting and worthwhile people to know. We are not alone in loving them.

MORE WAITING

After the emotional high of the social and raising all the money, we sent a triumphant cheque in, wrote the thank you cards, and then went back to waiting.

We waited for three years. The people who had rallied to our aid would routinely ask if we'd heard anything. One day, as I was walking down a side road to pick the boys up from school, a car pulled up beside me and a total stranger said, "You get the dog yet?" The community was INVESTED. I, who had such a hard time asking for help in the first place, felt terrible. I WANTED to have a dog to show the people who had given money. I WANTED that dog and Noah to be the perfect ending to a heartfelt story. But all I had was a gnawing sense of worry that there was never going to be a dog. When we flew to Ontario on a family trip, we actually drove out to the kennel to make sure the whole thing wasn't a scam. I got to touch the dogs. They were real. They were so close. It was all I could do to back away without stuffing one of them into my carry-on bag.

And then reality hit.

We got a call in October, three years and five months after our application. The dogs were ready. Our name was at the top of the list. Could I fly out in 14 days for a week of training? Time lurched. Three years of radio silence, then two weeks to prepare, pack, arrange childcare and work schedules, and then... off and running. A week of intense training (for me) in Ontario. A week to introduce the dog to Noah and transition into Winnipeg life. Then a public access test in a mall, a photo, a friendly goodbye and we were on our own.

Beau was a great dog. I had hoped for a chocolate lab, but Beau was yellow with a chocolate nose. He loved stuffies as much as Noah, but never fought for Baby Tiger. In his purple "working" jacket, he was quiet, calm and stoic. When we took his jacket off, he was goofy and fun. He loved to roll in the grass, but especially in snow. On walks, he'd spend half the time nose down, paddling along like a penguin. Noah loved to rest his head on Beau. He loved to look at his teeth. He loved holding a stick out and making Beau jump for it.

After six months, we made a slow transition to school. Noah was in grade six and he would be moving to a new school for grade seven. He would be leaving his friends and starting a segregated program for people with cognitive delays. It was important for me to have the kids who had seen Noah in the wheelchair, who had come to the fundraiser, finally have the experience of seeing Noah with his dog before they went separate ways. The transition was great. Everything was great.

Beau attended the symphony with us. A few concerned looks when the drum got going, but otherwise he settled marvelously. He came to church and went forward with Noah for communion (no, he didn't receive anything, though I bet he hoped someone would be sloppy with the crumbs). We went to movies, walked in the Santa Clause Parade, got featured on Shaw TV, and smiled at by passers-by. Everyone loves a dog and his boy.

DIAGNOSIS AT THE DOG PARK

I don't know who says that kids are open-minded and accepting; that children are, by nature, welcoming of diversity. I have not seen evidence of this. Kids, if anything, have a better understanding of pack mentality than adults who have had years of political correctness ingrained, as well as enough bumps along the road to realize that accommodation and compassion are also useful to the survival of the species.

Our church has been very supportive and welcoming to Noah. And people were thrilled that we brought our service dog to church with us. Nothing warms the cockles of our hearts more than to see the combined optics of purple dog and flappy boy move into the circle of communion. It speaks to us of how we want to be, how we imagine the world could be. It also speaks to each of our own insecurities—our own realization that, in each of us, there is a disabled part, a shameful inadequacy. If our community can expand to include the likes of Noah, then surely it might also be a place where we can bring our own quirky bits. Diversity is like a big group-trust exercise, a slow dance of vulnerability and acceptance, where we collectively learn to reach past what is comfortable, into an unsteady but grace-filled space.

Children, bless them, have not come to this place yet. They are still working primarily with their reptilian brains of survival. At our last church retreat, a five-year-old watched Noah for a few minutes and then turned to me and said, "There's something not quite right about this one." His brain was just getting used to what to expect, and Noah was a breach in the system—a flaw in the design. The great thing about kids is that they are highly teachable, so I replied, "you're absolutely right. His brain works differently," and the five-year-old nodded, reached up three feet to pat Noah on the head and let the issue go.

Some parents go weird when they see this kind of interaction and say, "No, Noah's just like everyone else." They say this so that their children will treat him with the respect of a peer, but kids have a shit detector that is too honed for this simple scheme. We can all see that Noah is different. Let's give kids that much. Then we can say, "Yes, he's different. And he's also a little bit the same. He doesn't talk very much, but he really likes cheeseburgers and drawing." There is permission to say, yes, your view of normal doesn't allow for this. Maybe it's time for your view of normal to expand and become a little more complex.

Every weekend, I take Noah and his dog, Beau, to the dog park. There's a big open field for the dogs to play and Noah loves running around. We let Beau run around with the other dogs for a while, then head down a trail that loops by the river.

Last week, we had a run-in that happens every once in a while. Sometimes the dogs are too focused on playing with each other to notice, but this time there was a black and white dog that got fixated on Noah. Noah likes to skip more than walk, and when he's happy, he makes a really sweet sound that is as contented as a cat purring. This one dog felt it was his obligation to let everyone know that there was a kink in the system. Just like the five-year-old boy, the dog was clearly saying, "This one's not quite right!" in his barking way. He attracted the attention of ten other dogs, and soon we were in the middle of a ring of dogs all barking at us. Some were clearly warning, and others simply wanted Noah to play with them. All were VERY clearly singling us out as only a pack of non-politically-correct canines can do. Beau was the only dog on the field ignoring us, clearly unimpressed with the novelty of the situation. Fortunately for us, Noah loves barking, so he was thrilled. All of the owners were mortified and were trying to call their dogs off and pretend things were normal. I felt partly like I'd been caught with my skirt tucked into my pantyhose at a party, and partly realizing the hilarity of the situation—that awkward funny that made me feel like my life was an episode on, "Curb Your Enthusiasm."

Eventually, the pack of dogs moved on and we continued our walk, with only the black and white dog left, trailing along like toilet paper on my shoe.

I thought this might be the best way for parents to get a diagnosis for their children. Neurologists and child psychologists are so conflict avoidant—so nervous to tell you that there might be something wrong with your child that it feels like pulling teeth to get a diagnosis. But put your kid in the middle of a pack of dogs and they'll let you know right away if something is amiss. It's a no-holds-barred, cost-effective way of separating the typical from the rest.

There is something so refreshing, so honest about children and animals. True diversity can only arise from this stark reality—something IS different about this one, and he's going to need a bit of help to integrate. The false honesty of the politically-correct position (we're all the same and we can all fit in together) is simply conflict avoidance and will not get us past the initial discomfort and into any opportunity for real relationship or understanding

SPEAKING FOR SOMEONE

Noah has a business, a Facebook page, and has been a featured (non) speaker at our local Pecha Kucha night. How, you may ask, has he built up such an empire without the help of language, social skills or caring about other people?

It seems as though he may have an active, meddling stage mother.

Let me explain.

When Noah was in grade five, we did a fair bit of traveling. Maybe we had our cameras out more than usual, maybe he was just ready for it, but for whatever reason Noah started getting fascinated with cameras. When we got back from our first trip, Hawaii, we had over 1,000 pictures on our memory card that he had taken. We stopped at Vancouver Island on the way home to see David's family for the holidays and Noah took another 300 photos just of the angel on the top of the Christmas tree. My mom-in-law saw him at work and commented that she hadn't even noticed that the angel had a face before. Hundreds more photos were taken in Edmonton where we went to see my dad, and more on our train ride back to Winnipeg.

As we looked at the photos, we saw themes emerging—perspectives that we hadn't considered before. Noah was obsessed with fences, stairwells and disappearing lines (when roads or fences disappear with perspective). He also loved to take pictures so close up that you couldn't tell what they were—they just became a study of texture and colour. He loved holding things up to the light and documenting how different things acted as a filter. He also liked to insert himself and his favourite stuffy, Baby Tiger, into shots. The pictures fascinated us. We began to see parallels between his pictures and how he made sense of the world.

A few people approached us to see his work (including a complete stranger on the train who then offered to build a website for Noah.) The pictures seemed to be the bridge that we needed to link Noah's world with our own. A static picture held enough of Noah's big, colourful, zany world to hold your attention, but made it seem manageable. A lot of his pictures are really beautiful. Many people (myself included) changed the way they take pictures after seeing Noah's work. Like, I didn't know you could shoot that landscape from the perspective of the grass, or hey, what would it look like if a plastic water bottle filtered your world and not just your drink?

At first it was cute, then it was annoying (hard to find the five shots you took because they're interspersed with 500 photos of exit signs). But no matter what we thought of it, Noah took his work so seriously that it demanded our respect. He will spend hours setting up a shot, trying different techniques, working from crazy angles. He bites his tongue in concentration and focuses in. If you see him at work, you can have your own opinion of the outcome, but you will have to acknowledge that he is a working artist, not a child with a toy.

As a way of sharing these photos, I got them printed on to note cards with a little description of Noah on the back. If this was the window into Noah's world, I wanted it to be accessible to people, and I also wanted to use his work as a means of financial independence in the future. As Noah grew in confidence with his cameras however, it became more of an effort to sustain his newfound hobby. When you are a true artist, you just have to submerge your (non-waterproof) camera in the water to fully explore the fountain out front. You would obviously need to see what kind of picture would appear whilst hurling your camera from your tree fort. It would become apparent that you'd need to tape your camera to a rake and set it up for crane shots. And of course, you would need to examine the effect of trying a long pan shot from the vantage point of inside a microwave with a revolving bottom. (Word up: it won't go well. There will be electrical sparks and then quite a bit of yelling.)

It was a good thing that the cards sold pretty well, because we had to replace our camera, as well as Grandma's and one from a very understanding respite worker.

With the cards, I tried hard to act as the bridge between worlds. I have had the privilege of seeing thousands of his photos (also the privilege of learning about the limits of my computer's memory). How do you encapsulate a flavour of the whole of Noah's work with one simple image?

I have always been wary of speaking for Noah. When we were teaching intraverbal sentences (sort of memorized responses to standard questions like, "what's your name?" or "what's your phone number?"—we started with the standard questions that a 911 worker would ask if by chance he was, hypothetically, found in the river or trying to get onto the roof of the legislative building.) I was careful to consider any response that might have some subjectivity to it. In answering, "How are you?" for example—would I teach him to always say, "I'm fine" even if he was yelling in anger? We settled on, "I'm good. And you?" What would be the answer to "What's your favourite colour?" We did a colour preference test before teaching him a rote answer (Blue). Then we realized that he had a tendency of colouring pictures and it seemed that his favourite people ended up pink or red and his least favourites were covered in blue marker. His EA had a pink face and blue arms, making us think he'd enjoy her more if she stopped thwarting his escape plans all the time. So, when he grabbed the blue marker in the colour preference test, was he saying he liked the colour or that he was annoyed with the test in general? No way of knowing.

I want to provide words for Noah to pave the way for other people to understand him. But I don't have a sure way of knowing that the words I choose are ones that are correct. The best we've got is my interpretation. Which is why, when I found a picture of me that had been coloured blue, I quickly surmised that blue now denoted people he secretly adored. Of course.

I want to find the balance between thinking that Noah is the magical unicorn child who is full of deep meaning, and that Noah's actions are random and meaningless. So I approached the descriptions of the photos with trepidation. I noticed that he frequently likes to look up the side of objects (like walls and fences) to the blue sky above and that he often does the same thing in life—I look at obstacles head-on, but he just tilts his head and sees beyond, giving him a generally cheerful disposition. There is one picture he took by putting the camera inside of Baby Tiger (of course the stuffy has been eviscerated and is more of a pelt than anything) and taking a self-portrait, which combined the tiger fur and his own face. I remain deeply suspicious that he feels he is part tiger. (In many family photos, he will sneak Baby Tiger up to his mouth so that his eyes peering over the Tiger are the only things you can see of his face, revealing his true tigerish identity. It's very covert.) In others, I just note that his perspective is so different that everyday objects appear foreign to us, which is a way of showing me that many of the elements of everyday life that I expect him to recognize are foreign to him.

In any case, I try as much as possible to stay out of the way of his work because people are generally really happy to find a point of recognition or connection to him. After getting the cards printed, a friend of mine who is a designer asked if I would share his work at a conference of other designers (an event called Pecha Kucha) and so I went as his spokesperson, while he jumped on stage, excitedly taking pictures of the slides of his pictures that were projected as I spoke. And of course, because there were so many photographers there, many people took pictures of him taking pictures of his own pictures and the whole experience was very Meta.

We started a Flickr account and a Facebook page to show Noah's photos and sell his cards. He has 300 people following him on Facebook and a bunch of the people from Pecha Kucha night follow him on Flickr.

Shortly after Pecha Kucha, Noah started a time of exploration of printing out his pictures, gluing them to the fence and basketball net in the backyard and then taking pictures of his collages. He also got really interested in videography, especially taking videos of things in the dark while shouting. These artistic endeavours were not as readily acknowledged in the artistic community. I found it fascinating to watch him build his collages, print them, cut pieces out, colour them and then add them to the growing wall of work. He was, above all, not interested in producing work that would match the couch. But his work was also no longer riding the sacred balance between the worlds—he was veering pretty far into his own planet and suddenly it wasn't the beautiful work that people loved. Four hundred pictures of drywall is just not interesting to anybody, even if there are carefully-documented changes in light and tape placement in each of them.

Recently, Noah did a series of drawings on the computer. They were weird and colourful and intense. I wasn't sure what his newfound fans would think, but I chose six of them to turn into cards and they sold out right away. I loved this—people were willing to step out of their comfort zones and appreciate his stuff. The balance between the worlds wasn't quite as rigid as I had thought. These cards brought out more emotion from people. It wasn't the, "Oh, that's beautiful," kind of response, but more like, "that's so crazy, I love it." I think it also reflects a change in me—not quite as interested in trying to get Noah to fit into a mold, or make him acceptable, but instead celebrating his weirdness, and enjoying the more wild and wooly world that he's from.

Over the years, he has lost his love for photography. And because of a strange miscommunication, he no longer enjoys drawing pictures on my computer. I thought I was doing something great by downloading a movie on to the computer, but he was traumatized by it (the same movie that he has watched at my mom's every week for the last year and a half), but now he is scared to come into my office, even though I showed him that I've deleted the movie and emptied the trash. For the last year, if I want him to set foot in my office, we have to do a little ritual in which he says, It's ok?" and I have to say, "It's ok!" Then he will stay for up to five minutes, but even then he is usually reaching in to use the computer with his feet still outside the threshold.

Noah has begun a new series of drawings. He draws at least six pictures a day of the Aquatech kids; variations of a poster that hung at our local swimming pool for a few years. He has loved that poster for nine years and to this day, when we go to the pool, we still have to go and observe the (now blank) wall and point out that the kids used to be there. We have gone to the Aquatech store and the staff recognize us. They gave Noah a t-shirt a few years ago that thrilled him, and his educational assistants once got him a t-shirt with the Aquatech slogan, "We've got your pool!" on it. It was the first sentence he ever learned to read. That's also how he learned to use Google maps—he wanted to visit the Aquatech store more frequently than we felt the staff would remain friendly. With Google maps he could spend hours looking at the sign from the virtual road.

We now have a bag at the front door with about 200 drawings of the Aquatech kids. These drawings are only taken to grandma's house. She gets the honour of having one- -and-a-half walls covered floor to ceiling with these drawings and copious amounts of tape. The walls are a few inches thick in areas, because he adds new work every week.

He also has started a binder with index cards. For many months, each card had a picture based on a similar theme. They all had what looked like him in bed with his striped blanket and a gigantic black rectangle floating over top of his body. Each of these cards is titled "Don't be Scared!" (Noah labels the pictures on his own). Not worrying at all to a mother. I don't know how to explain these photos. He takes them to Mom's house every week too. He lays them precisely on the floor of the bedroom and shines a flashlight over them, shouting a monologue from, "Thomas the Tank Engine" or "Casper's Haunted Christmas."

His new series is electric blue, jagged lines and flashes of other colour. It's called, "Speakers! Big Loud Roar!"

I'm beginning to see that some of his work needs to be shared; others are just for his own benefit. The more he expresses himself through his art, the more I simply can't catch up. I appreciate it, but I can't be the bridge any longer. Maybe it can speak for itself. Maybe that's not the point of his art.

THE VERY BEST DAY

Parents were squished into lines of fold-up metal chairs in the main gym. Streamers taped to the wall. Slowly shuffling in was the Grade Six graduating class of 2010, proud, awkward and excited. Every parent stood to take a picture, every child was a celebrity.

Noah's EAs had decided he should be as independent as possible, so Noah walked in without an adult to guide him. Occasionally, one of the other kids would reach out and put a hand on his shoulder to remind him not to jump, or to get him to follow in line.

I had worked for three weeks to make Noah agree to wear jeans for this occasion. Somehow, his normal uniform of baggy sweatpants that were three inches too short did not match the solemnity of the occasion. No, today he was bedecked in green runners, skinny jeans, a cool t-shirt and a short sleeve plaid button-up shirt worn undone overtop. He had questioned this additional layer in the morning—he thinks it is ridiculous to wear two shirts at once. He looks at you like he's trying to figure out if you're running the "what's wrong" program, where you intentionally put a shoe on your head and see if he notices. But today I convinced him that it was a two-shirt day. And if he felt his mother was being a little too bossy about the clothes, a little too fussy about the hair, he shared those same emotions with his older brother, who had endured his mother's attentions for grade six grad two years before. This time it wasn't about the autism. Graduations just bring out the crazy in mothers.

The kids had been asked to prepare a one-sentence remark about their favourite memory of school. When my older son had gone through this, I hadn't even asked ahead of time what he would say. But Noah's team had been working on his sentence for the last two months. We first had to decide what his answer would realistically be. We drew pictures about different things and showed a few photos. He seemed to respond most to a memory about when the grade five and six classes had gone to camp, so we decided his sentence would be, "when we tipped the canoe at camp." Over the last two months, we had been teaching him this sentence.

The kids were in line, taking turns walking up to the mic, saying their favourite memory and then receiving their diploma. Finally it was Noah's turn. Again, the EAs wanted him to be independent, so they sent him up with his buddy, Sammy. Sammy held the mic while Noah, a little too close, a little too eager, said, "WHENWETIPPEDTHE CANOEATCAMP." It made perfect sense to those of us who had been working on it for the last few months, but fairly unintelligible to the rest of the parents. Sammy, enjoying his role as interpreter, said, "My buddy, Noah, here, says his favourite memory is when he tipped over in a canoe at camp." As he was saying this, I could clearly see that Noah was making a quick assessment of the distance between himself and his EAs, the relatively small size of Sammy and his own desperate need to make use of this golden opportunity. After a brief struggle, he wrestled the mic free from Sammy and yelled, "SURRENDER NOW!" into the mic. Pleased with himself, he happily handed the mic to the principal. The crowd paused momentarily to take in the spectacle, and then burst into applause.

"SURRENDER NOW!" has become an anthem for Noah. When given the opportunity, this message is the most important one to shout. Just last fall, when he was the ring bearer at our family friend and respite worker, Laurel's wedding, he got a similar glint in his eye as he came forward to give the pastor the rings. Again, he noticed how simple it would be to wrestle the mic free from the unassuming pastor. With only one of his hands free (I was holding the other—but alas, had made an unfortunate decision to wear heels and was pegged into the grass and a little too slow with my reactions), Noah chucked the useless cargo of rings, grabbed the mic and repeated his plea for surrender. Totally appropriate for an impromptu wedding address.

Five years ago, I would have been mortified. Either my dignity has been permanently scarred, or I have finally come to the understanding that there is no need to apologize for my boy being who he is. Both times, the people who knew Noah burst out laughing and let the moment pass. His intrusion didn't colour the entire event, but it did help inform people more about how he interacts with the world. And for our dear respite worker, Laurel, who cannot discuss her job with her friends because of the Personal Health Information Act, it provided a small window into her life and the people she works with.

At both the wedding and Noah's grad event, I got a glimpse into Noah's future, where he would be allowed to be himself within a community that was stable enough to absorb him. I have worked hard at getting Noah to act appropriately and think about others, and the world seems to be working hard to embrace the eccentricities and requirements of the Noah's in our midst. For all of the global warming and Tea Party and economic recession that seem to point to a dismal future, I also have hope that we are, in small ways, learning to become human.

As soon as Noah is finished shouting "SURRENDER NOW!" he relinquishes the mic and struts proudly back to his seat. He has accomplished his mission. The rest of the festivities, whether it is a wedding or grad ceremony, carry on to their conclusion. But Noah's smile of accomplishment lingers long after the event, and he will happily act out this story for days after if you ask him about it and pretend to hold a mic up to his mouth.

After the grad ceremony, the gym transforms for the school dance. The budget has clearly not allowed for a light show, but several moms have brought in coloured lights that spin and someone has a smoke machine. Big speakers are installed and the music fills the space. The girls are giggling, awkward in their first pair of high heels and shiny with lip-gloss. At first I worry that Noah won't fit in, but all the boys are running wildly in the gym, over-stimulated by hormones, music, the shock of these shiny girls they've never noticed before.

The girls are quickly realizing that these boys are not the ones of their dreams—the ones who will ask them to dance, who will acknowledge in any meaningful way that they exist. They are the same stinky, bouncing boys who have traveled through all of elementary school with them. The kids form a makeshift circle and take turns throwing people into the centre ring. Somebody grabs Noah and throws him into the middle. He pauses a minute, looking a little stunned. All the kids start chanting, "Go, Noah! Go Noah!" and someone shouts, "Do the Noah dance" and they all start hopping and flapping. Noah smiles and joins in. All of the parent chaperones are in tears. This is parenting done well. The kids are used to Noah— them doing his flappy dance has nothing to do with mockery and everything to do with recognition. This is how he rolls.

It's a really beautiful moment and it is still engrained in my mind. This beautiful moment of inclusion and connection.

A few seconds later, Noah breaks free and continues his loping laps around the gym. The kids move on to other dance games, unaware of the adults around them still clinging to each other. Next year, these kids will move on to junior high. Noah will not be able to stay with them. The gap is too great. It is time for him to run with the special needs class, to find himself with neurological peers.

But this day, he found himself in a circle of friends, celebrating the long haul that was elementary. He will come home with memories of being able to drink unlimited pop and eat chips. Of big speakers and loud music. The thought of his inclusion doesn't thrill him. It is immaterial to him. Those kids have come to love and appreciate Noah. He has learned to tolerate them. But we return home full up. It has been the very best day.

In 24 hours, we will be in line at Old Navy, buying a change of clothes and heading to a hotel because our house has been consumed by fire. We will begin the most difficult year of our lives—a year that will come near to breaking all of us.

But we don't know that yet. We soak in the very best day and sleep deeply, thinking that life doesn't get better than this.

FIRE

It was Friday afternoon. Almost 4:00pm. I was sitting on the couch by the window reading a magazine. David and Jase were at the chiropractor. Noah had just arrived home from his final full day of school and was taping his artwork to the walls in the storage room. Summers are often difficult for us because of a lack of childcare, but I had decided to focus solely on being at home with the boys. It was going to be a big transition into high school for both of them, so I didn't want to be stressed about anything.

I was checking on Noah about every ten minutes, enjoying the fact that he was playing independently. The last few months had been the first in our lives that Noah was allowed to play on a different floor than where we were. He had earned that trust over a long time. Just as I was about to go down to check again, Noah had run upstairs to get his portable DVD player, so I didn't bother going down. It was just about time to do another check.

And then I heard Noah roar.

It was a bigger sound than I'd ever heard him make. Both the dog and I stiffened. As I stood up, my heart sank.

Something was very off. I felt heat in the floor as I walked across the room to the basement stairs.

I went downstairs to see a wall of flames to my left, where the storage area was. Noah was in front of it, jumping up and down, yelling, eyes mad with light. I thought of water. Of fire extinguishers. The wall seemed impenetrable. So I yelled, "Get out of there" and pulled Noah upstairs. I grabbed the phone and called 911. "There's a fire!" I yelled, giving my address in full panic mode. "Are you in the house now?" asked the operator. "If your house is on fire, you should get out of the house," she continued in a stunning bit of logic. I tried to explain that the fire was downstairs and I was ok on the main floor and then the line went dead. I realized that the fire might not stay in the basement for long.

Noah was super amped, eyes still bright and now he was shouting "GETOUTTATHERE!!!" over and over, mimicking the panic in my voice. I grabbed him and the dog, pausing momentarily at the door, willing my brain to respond somehow. I took our wedding album, remembering that our photographer had retired years before and I wouldn't be able to replace it. I will never live this down. As sweet as that thought was, I can only say—in case of fire, remember the following things:
- Shoes
- Keys
- Computers

Because without these things, you're going to start feeling like a complete idiot once the adrenaline wears off, and you're holding on to a fake wood-paneled photo album that won't start the car or work as trade for food. Also, a leash for the dog is handy in emergencies, so try not to forget that.

I run outside and see my neighbour having a beer on the porch. His face is relaxed and he's digging the fact that the weekend has begun and it takes a minute for him to register that I'm having a completely different experience. He calls 911 for me.

Just as I hear the fire engines sirens, I see that David and Jase have returned from the chiropractor. I'm yelling for David to move the car for the fire trucks to get in. He is paralyzed for a minute. Later, he tells me that he's trying to figure out what's happening. I've got my "Noah's in danger" panic face on, but he sees Noah right next to me, so he doesn't absorb the fact that something else could be wrong until he looks up to the house and sees smoke billowing out of the windows. Suddenly, he moves into action and backs the car out of the way. The fire fighters come in and do their thing.

Noah's still yelling, so we put him in the car with Jase to keep him out of the way and safe. Big mistake. Jase is in the car watching the smoke flood out of his bedroom window, grieving all of his beloved books and all of his writing, while his younger brother is flying higher than a kite. Sibling bonding is not being deepened.

One neighbour, whose daughter has worked with Noah in Special Olympics, takes Noah into her house and we see him trying to watch the fire out the living room window, smiling and jumping, but (blessedly) muted by the glass. The neighbour on the other side slides a pair of sandals on to my feet, so relieved that it's not her house, yet feeling guilty for the relief.

The fire chief stands next to us, coaching us through the fire. "Now the smoke has gone from black to white. That's a good sign. It means they've stopped the source and we're over the worst of it." There are lots of questions, and people are gathering. Was it electrical? Do you smoke? Were there lighters in the house? Do you know what happened?

My mind is pounding and it feels like I'm standing near a waterfall. All I can hear is accusation and blame, I'm bouncing back and forth between self-loathing that I should have been checking more and it's my fault, and MY KID JUST BURNED DOWN MY HOUSE and wondering if he would get charged for arson. "He didn't mean to," I keep saying to the chief, who seems to have an enormous skill for being around people who are losing their minds. I hope I'm right. Repeating it doesn't make it go away, but it beats in my mind over and over like a metronome. He didn't mean to. He didn't mean to. Maybe if I say it enough, it will be true.

I realize that my friend is having a team party and meeting for her child who is also autistic, just down the street. We share many of the same respite people and I know Noah would be safe there. They know how to take care of him and they might have a bit more objectivity in this situation—it's not their stuff going down in flames. David drives him over, and their party is in full swing. "Our house is on fire. Can you take Noah?" he says, killing the mood significantly for them. The team rolls with it and they are shaken, but fine to take Noah.

We spend an hour at the house, answering questions, sweet-talking the fire chief to go in and find wallets and shoes before they lock the place up for the weekend. There are still toxic fumes in the house that are preventing them from doing a full investigation. They will return Monday morning. Until then, the house is boarded up and padlocked and we are told to go to a hotel.

We make our way back to our friends, who have ordered pizza and have lots more questions. We find friends who will take Jase. We call our parents, most of whom are out of province and have never sounded further away. We buy a change of clothes and toothbrushes. David turns to me and says, "This might take all summer to recover," not knowing then that it would be a full year until we would be able to move back and even longer before recovery would be possible.

After the weekend, we discover what happened. Noah had taped one of his drawings on to the track light, which probably had a hotter bulb than it should have. The drawing caught fire and landed on a foam cushion, which ignited the storage room, and tunneled through to the heat ducts. The fire then travelled up to my office directly above, and the boys' rooms on the second floor. Noah had a spare mattress right up to the vent, which helped slow the fire in his room, but Jase's entire room, being small and full of books and paper, was consumed. In the end, all of the windows in the house would need to be replaced because the seals were broken, as well as all the drywall, lumber, floor boards and stucco. Anything that had plastic on it would need to be thrown out, though many things with metal were corroded and damaged as well. In the end, we lost 99% of our belongings.

.

WHAT NOT TO WEAR

The evening of the fire, wedged between the pizza debrief and shock with friends, and the first sleep of many away from home, we needed to get a hold of a few necessities. David deposited the boys and me at Old Navy to get clothing staples while he went off to hunt and gather toothbrushes and such. The idea was to pick up the bare minimum. However, with four people, all needing underwear, socks, shoes, pajamas and clothes, the list was daunting. We would need one outfit each for when we were outside and at least one cozy outfit each as we adapted to an air-conditioned hotel. And, because the hotel has a pool and we had no other toys, books or distractions, we'd need swimsuits.

As a student of the show "What Not to Wear", I was very aware that clothes affect the way you feel. I was also aware that you absolutely MUST try on clothes to see if they work for your body. I knew the rule that capri pants are friends to no one. However, all the shopping montages on TV featured a woman who spent all week in New York with two cheerleading fashion experts at her side, totally devoted to helping her find her fashion style. My companions in this scenario were two shell-shocked, sooty teenagers.

This was no time for flattering clothes. It was no time to honour the request of a socially conscious teenager who preferred organic, sweatshop-free clothing. It was a survival mission - the only goal was to avoid public nudity. I grabbed the clothes required for four people in the time it took David to get four toothbrushes, manly deodorant, a hairbrush, and a very large container of Advil.

This was my uniform for the next two weeks:

Hair - Having just gotten a short, arty, faux hawk that required some fairly specific hair products, my hair quickly devolved to an exact replica of Donald Trump.

Face - no makeup (now questioning why the husband was in charge of toiletries), with the added bonus of red, runny eyes. My glasses were recovered after the fire and the thick plastic rim was smoke damaged, resulting in chronic allergies.

Shirt - A seafoam blue t-shirt which turned out to be surprisingly thin and see through (I should have avoided the $5 bargain bin.)

Pants - Grey capri pants (I know! Either them or booty shorts, which even Stacy and Clinton would have advised against.)

Shoes - Red and Green flip flops (two pairs for $10!).

Underwear - Ill-fitting. One should never buy skivvies under pressure.

To top it off, I soon discovered that the bathing suit I bought was maternity. Definitely not an ego booster on the water slide. I mentioned this on Facebook and got a teasing comment from a sister-in-law suggesting it might be a sign that it was time to expand the family.

Hahaha... No.

The thing to get through this summer was not going to involve morning sickness. I think my ovaries were too clenched to even consider the scenario. Besides, living in a hotel room with two teenagers and a dog in the same room does not lead to baby-making magic, trust me.

It seems so small, so petty, to mourn clothing. My clothes weren't even that great. But they did give me a sense of identity. The leather jacket I found a few months before, my boiled wool coat from Northern Ireland. Handmade leather jewelry that I valued. I missed the stories that went with them. I missed the pleasure of wearing familiar colours and textures - the soft knit shirt, the cozy warm sweater.

After two weeks, my friend's fashion-conscious teenage son finally broke from the pain of seeing us wear the same clothes and came over with a bag of his own castoffs for the boys. He had also convinced his dad to donate a few shirts to save David from a bright striped golf-shirt that had seemed less annoying when I bought it two weeks before.

A friend of my sister dropped off a bag of clothes for me. She worded it gracefully, but effectively she was donating all the clothes she couldn't fit anymore after losing weight. I was grateful for alternatives to my see-through shirt, but it was a special kind of something for my ego wearing another person's fat clothes.

It was a reverse makeover - an individual rendered into a generic, frazzled lady with a combover and falling arches (damned flip flops!)

I believe that things are not as important as people. But I know that things can also help people remember who they are.

SOMETIMES I DON'T WANT TO BE GRATEFUL

About two months after the fire, we were just getting settled into our new temporary house. Noah was out with a fairly new respite worker and I was glad for the chance to work on the insurance claim. When my cell phone rang, I got a shiver of adrenaline—in my experience cell phones never bring good news. I shook my head, took a deep breath and reminded myself that sometimes a cell phone is just a cell phone.

I answered. Turns out I was right to fear the call. It was the respite worker, telling me that everything was fine, but there was an incident and could I meet him at the hospital. Apparently Noah jumped into the river at the Forks and needed to be rescued by the police, several citizens and a couple of water taxi employees.

A flurry of plans and then I'm off to the hospital. Noah is still in a hospital bed, ostensibly being treated for potential hypothermia. The respite worker is off to the side, looking pretty grey and rattled. It's clear who the victim of today's events has been. I fill out the last of the paperwork and both the hospital and police release us. I charitably give the respite worker the rest of the day off. Just before getting out of the car, he says, "I thought you should know—there were reporters at the site, so Noah might be in the news tonight."

I had called David on my way to the hospital, but now that everything's fine, I don't want him to know or else he'll be distracted the rest of the day. He calls back to check-in at lunch, but I evasively say, "I'll talk to you more when you get home, but everything is fine here." What I don't know is that once I hang up, he turns on the radio and hears a shocking report of a teenager in the river who needed rescue. It doesn't take a rocket scientist to put two and two together.

The news reports go on every half hour. They are saying Noah is three years older than he really is. There is no mention of a diagnosis. People are speculating about this delinquent. It's so dehumanizing. I need to name it on Facebook. And soon, I get a call from a news station asking for an interview (Winnipeg is a small enough city that there is only one relation removed from my friend list to a reporter).

I decide that if Noah is going to be highlighted on the news tonight, I want to control how he is discussed. The reporter comes over and I stress that this incident is a result of our recent loss of funding. Hey, if I'm going to look like a crap mother on TV, I might as well bring the government down with me. I try to paint the picture of what kind of support Noah needs, how this is a daily fear of mine.

Over the next two days, as I sit with reporters for TV and radio, I try to keep the focus on the need for funding and support. However, they all want to turn this into a miracle story. How lucky it was that people were around and how horrible it would be if Noah had died. That we are grateful and this will never happen again. That Noah has learned his lesson.

They don't want to hear that Noah has been higher than a kite since the incident. That he loved seeing himself on TV the first night. That this is not the first time that our boy has put himself in mortal danger, or that there is a great likelihood that this will happen again. Nobody wants to know that living with Noah means being prepared every day to get a phone call saying that he died.

I DO say I'm grateful. And I am. But I have been grateful to random strangers for saving my boy's life for a decade now. There are so many people to thank. And I'm even more grateful for the people who choose to spend time with him on a weekly basis—my respite team, Noah's EA's, my mother. What I'd prefer is to be less grateful to people during a crisis and more grateful for structures and funding that will prevent Noah from getting into those crises in the first place.

But that's too hard a story to tell. I try to tell as much to one of the reporters. I say that, while I'm so grateful for the people who jumped in to save Noah, I still feel like I'm in over my head and just hoping that the government will jump in and save me. The truth is, this same scenario might play out again tomorrow if something doesn't change. This wasn't a freak accident. It is part of the rhythm of our life.

This is not a time to ask for more, but to humbly say thank you, it will never happen again. From the comments that people add to the news reports, I see I'm whiny and my kid should be institutionalized. Sigh. Note to self: never read the comments underneath any article on the web.

There have been times in the past when I have bonded with Noah's protectors. There are a few people from the neighbourhood who have seen me completely devastated and have been there to bring Noah home. It's not even that we've become friends—but we have a bond that links our stories together. This event is different. It's so soon after the house fire, when I had to rely on friends and relative strangers to come and sort out every single item that's been lost. To go through all of my drawers and label each one of the books I owned, each box of treasures hidden in the basement. David's workplace has been bringing over meals once a week. My respite team has seen me in tears too often this summer. I just can't open myself up to more people. My body can't process the reality of what almost happened. I wasn't at the riverside watching his blonde head float away, yelling for people to help.

All I want is for the incident to go away, to grab hold of the hint of normalcy we were within grasp of before this happened. But I dutifully write thank-you cards to each of the rescuers. They are good people, worthy of heartfelt thanks.

Six months later, I get a phone call from a news station letting me know that Noah's four rescuers are getting awards for saving him. They put me back on TV, asking how grateful I am. "SOO grateful," I say. "Can you imagine what your life would be like if they didn't save him? If he had died that day?" Yes, I think. I imagine that every time my phone rings. Every time he is five minutes late coming home with a respite worker. "I would be devastated," I say.

One person was especially helpful in the rescue. He was a random jogger passing by who was stopped by my respite worker. This man jumped on the water taxi and quickly assessed that Noah was autistic, explaining to the police why his behaviour was off, why he wasn't grabbing the life preserver. He knew because his own son is autistic—just a few years older than Noah. I felt a particular connection to this man and had written him that summer, but I hear now that his wife wants to connect.

I friend her on Facebook and see that she's posted pictures of her husband getting the award. Her friends have commented on it, mentioning again that they hope, "that boy's family is grateful."

We try a few back and forth messages, getting to know each other. But all we have in common is a desperate love for our boys and the trauma of being related to someone involved in the incident at the river. I have nothing left. I cannot reach out anymore. The events of the last year have been devastating on a number of levels, but right now, I'm so exposed. I need to retreat, to grow back some dignity. I stop writing messages.

A few months pass and I wonder how this woman is doing. I think I may have enough in the tank for another try at our relationship. When I look her up on Facebook, though, I see she has unfriended me.

There have been times when I have actually been the good mother, the supportive friend, the kind stranger who reaches out. I am sad to think that this woman has received the paralyzed, demanding, unsatisfying part of me. I feel like this whole situation has been about failure.

There is something about gratitude that can't be forced. The more I try to force it, the smaller I become inside. I feel like somehow it's been tied to obligation. Living with Noah has taught me that life is not fair. Some people will demand more than others. And some debts cannot be paid back. The no-nonsense Mennonite part of me cannot accept this. We are raised to be givers, not receivers. People can rely on us, though we don't like to rely on others.

I hope one day that I can save someone's life, or do something heroic that will justify all of the help and support I have received. Or maybe I hope that I will one day be able to accept that there is abundant love and support for Noah (and for me) and I will be able to offer heartfelt thanks to the people who help us, with no shame in knowing that I will keep needing to ask for more.

PEACE

It is the end of a long day. A pool of light gathers around me as I stay up to read. This is precious time—I don't have to respond to anything, don't need to force interaction, don't need to manage. My book takes me into another world full of poetry and rushing water and wonder. Breath fills the room; the half-snore of my beloved next to me, the deep sighs of Noah, who is sleeping on the mat beside our bed. We had tried to keep him out for a few months, but then realized that, when the boy who was foretold not to care about you cries to come in and share your cozy space, you let him. His dog Beau lies at his feet, soft growls announcing the onset of a dream. The room is warm and I am full of love and gratitude. Tomorrow is another day, but it is not calling yet.

The Lord almighty, grant us a quiet night and a perfect end.

ONE STEP FORWARD

I was walking to Safeway with Noah to get a bag of chips. He was skipping happily along just in front of me. I marveled at how happy and free we both felt after a year full of trauma. I was so proud of him. A few years ago I wouldn't have let him walk without holding his hand. He had a tendency to run toward whatever distraction caught his attention.

As we approached the main street, I called out for him to stop. There were lots of cars, but I was sure he would listen. He had earned this independence. He took one more hop step before he stopped. A little closer to the road than I hoped, but still good. Sigh of relief.

As he turned to face me and wait for me to catch up, a man on a bike flew by on the sidewalk. As I caught up, the cyclist spun around and came back toward us, screaming and swearing. "He almost killed me. He came out of nowhere and I had to swerve into traffic. I could have fucking died! What's his problem? He was skipping like a goddamn idiot!"

I looked at my beautiful boy from his eyes. An idiot, a retard, rude and a threat.

"He's autistic, have some fucking compassion," I shot back. Maybe not the most gracious advocate.

One more circle around us and then the man sped off, flipping me the bird over his shoulder.

Stunned, I turned back to my boy, my sweet boy. Six foot two, but hardly verbal. Not understanding a lot of what was just said, but clearly knowing that he had done something wrong. "Bad!" he shouts, biting his hand. I gather him up in my arms and herd him through the crosswalk.

Our fun trip now clouded, we buy the damn chips and head home. I'm simultaneously trying to shake if off and plan my status update on Facebook, where I can vent all my anger and frustration. Not just at this cyclist. Some days I'm done with autism. I just want a simple happy day with no drama.

As we make our way through the parking lot, my hand clenched over my son's, I notice the same guy cycling toward us. I pull my boy close in, terrified of what's going to happen. This guy would have had to cross the street and wait for us. I scan quickly for witnesses in case things get physical.

He cycles steadily toward us and just before he passes he mutters, "I'm sorry. I didn't know." Speechless, I gape as he fades from sight, adrenaline draining from my body.

FROM BAD TO WORSE

Noah sleeps over at Gramma's house on Friday nights (blessed be she). Late in the evening, he had apparently discovered a large tub of Vaseline and covered himself in it. Mom had tried to get it out of his hair, but after three shampoos it wasn't moving and frankly, I think she was a bit daunted by the idea of recovering her bedspread and carpet. So he was sent back to us to deal with. After some research on Google, I dumped a box of baking soda on his head to absorb the grease. Somewhat subdued, Noah returned to colouring, as I continued to research next steps.

Fifteen minutes later, I realize that it's been quiet. Too quiet. I have been watching out of the corner of my eye, but I realize that Noah has been colouring, but it wasn't on paper. The dog walks by, looking at me beseechingly. Noah has tigerized him—coloured on hot pink stripes with a sharpie. I go to find him so I can yell at him and discover a boy with a green face and hands. This is what happens when you've got a kid stuck at the toddler stage of development. I surrender to defeat and document the chaos on Facebook. All of it is annoying, but it's also pretty funny. At least I didn't have plans for the day anyway.

I know I need to bathe the dog, but I can't walk him if he's wet. The walk needs to come first and I decide hot pink is "jaunty" on a dog. I cleverly throw a hat on Noah to cover the baking soda/Vaseline fiasco and a pair of sunglasses on myself (no one will ever guess who we are). I remind myself that dignity is over-valued and the three of us take our show on the road. Lady of mystery, Shrek and Pink Tiger together at last, heading to the park.

By the time we get there, I'm feeling good. There was an element of disaster, but fundamentally we're all fine. There's nothing to do but laugh and spend the rest of the day alternating between wet dog and wet boy. The dog rolls in the snow, leaving a rosy pink glow in his wake.

And then Noah snaps. He throws himself to the ground, face first, screaming. I'm stunned, not knowing where this energy came from. I let him cry it out for a bit, but then it's time to get it together and head home. I make him stand up and he charges at me, hands around my throat. He's screaming so hard that the blood vessels around his eyes break. My neck is bruised and I take a second to catch my breath. My toddler has become a threatening menace, a person I don't recognize at all. He has become the Incredible Hulk. There is no way I can control him.

There is a certain humility required to call my mother and have her come get us. As we wait for her car to come, I think about the times she's had to call us. I feel the sense of absolute failure and shame. The stark reality that I am not safe and it's this boy who I love who is the danger to me. I'm bewildered that the day has turned so suddenly. Weren't we just laughing and rolling our eyes at this scene?

My mother takes in the sight of green boy turned red from screaming. Woman of intrigue with tears streaming below the sunglasses. Pink dog cowering in the tennis court, too scared to come back to us. She hustles us into the car and drives us home.

I return to a bottle of wine on my front steps, left by a friend who saw my Facebook post. Many comments on the update, laughing and enjoying the hilarity of the pictures. That's the spirit I had when I put them up, but I can't comment on it now. Somehow the escapade at the park will not find its way onto my wall. I can't even put it into words. My baby is growing up. My baby hurt me. His anger and my fear have created a separation that feels irreparable. There is no funny way to comment on this, no irreverent "take" on what happened.

Of course, the bruises fade. The dog loses his stripes. Noah's hair returns to its former glory and both the green marker and the red from the bulging blood vessels disappear over time. My mom replaces her bedspread and carpet. But my heart takes a bit longer to heal. We are changing. This is both good and bad. God give me strength to face the man that Noah is becoming and let him not be a stranger to me.

ONE WEEKEND

Saturday morning:
Emergency call from respite workers. Noah overpowered two of them at the mall, waterskied them over to a record store (he was attached to a tether), turned the speakers up loud and shoplifted a DVD. Security stopped him and all was returned.

Debrief with respite workers.

Saturday, afternoon:
Dog park. Noah escaped two times to run up a hill and roll down adjoining cliff. Much jumping and yelling. Leash wrapped around Noah's waist to complete walk.

Medication given.

Saturday, evening:
Noah peed on mattress while masturbating. Four loads of laundry.

Meltdown in shower—in an effort to get a rise out of me, he learned to direct water through the moveable nozzle and doused room.

Medication given again.

Sunday, morning:
Report from respite worker. Noah poured juice on the counter at respite worker's house. While cleaning up, Noah had a meltdown and shoved worker out of the way, so she put him in a headlock and threw him to the ground. Her two dogs lay on him until he calmed down.

Mom came over for a meeting regarding her living will. Long discussion of executor responsibilities, and end-of-life decisions made.

Sunday, afternoon:
Noah returned home. I did a calming exercise with him to release energy. Calmed, I send Noah to the main floor and have a three-minute conversation with Jase.

Return to the main floor. Noah has disappeared.

Found a few minutes later in the basement. He had found a tube of A535 and applied it to half of his body.

He then plugged in the sauna and was trying to turn it on when I found him.

Heat reaction and toweling off.

Walk at the dog park. Subdued.

Sunday, evening:
Dog stepped on by stranger at church, yelping ensued. Noah had a mini meltdown at church. David on duty; managed to keep him in the pew until end of service. Eight pages of drawing and five pages ripped separately from a spiral bound notebook during the service.

Debriefing conversation. Decision made to include only loose-leaf paper in church bag in future.

Medication given.

10:30pm: Noah went to sleep

12:30am: Noah woke up and came to our room (he has a mat on the floor).

4am: Noah became obsessed with trying to unscrew the switch plate of the electrical outlet with his fingernail.

5am: Change of shift from Kalyn to David. Dog followed Kalyn to spare room and had a panic attack, which discouraged sleep for either party.

7am: Noah fell asleep.

8am: Kalyn fell asleep.

8:15am: Everyone woke up late. Noah showered, dressed and ready for school bus at 8:45am.

8:45am: Small emotional collapse by Kalyn. Showered, dressed and ready for appointment by 9:15am.

Four cups of coffee ingested by noon.

THE SHORTEST CHAPTER

Fuck it. I'm done with autism.

RELENTLESS

There is a natural rhythm to life. You breathe in, you breathe out, you work hard all week and you get to sleep in on the weekend. You can handle stress because you know you'll get a chance to crash later.

Autism messes with this rhythm. Effectively, it removes the lulls between the waves.

Kelley Jo Burke, a Canadian writer and mother of an autistic child says, "Autism isn't a bad life. It's just relentless." Exactly.

I'm writing this in the lobby of a movie theatre because I need to be here as support for my respite worker, who is watching a movie with Noah.

A month ago, Noah developed an obsession about moving back to the "Blue House," the place we lived for a year while we rebuilt our home. June is our toughest month— the respite workers change their schedules, teachers are wrapping-up, the rest of the school is abuzz with spring fever and the days are long (making bedtime too bright). Add to that our penchant for disasters happening in June— last minute changes in staffing that give me three days to create a viable plan for September, funding announcements that create havoc for plans, not to mention two major moves in June for the last two years—one after the fire into temporary and transient housing and then the move back to our rebuilt home. Everyone in our family goes a little twitchy in June, waiting for the anvil to drop, the stick of dynamite to be lit. Noah especially needs extra support.

One way he gets it is to lodge one thing in his mind and obsess over it. This June it was about the Blue House. None of us have good memories of that house, as it is associated with our most difficult year: daily meltdowns, endless insurance claims, the dog's panic attacks, financial instability. None of us were particularly jazzed about the idea of moving back, so Noah wasn't getting anything positive back when he kept asking for it. Using his ingenuity, he figured that the only way to get to the Blue House was through fire. I found him trying to set our thermostat on fire with the BBQ lighter and when he saw me, he said very nicely, "I want fire, please." ("Way to use your words, but HELL NO!") I needed a change of momentum, so I created a new obsession that was related to the memory, but still doable. I booked a hotel room for July 5, giving him something to look forward to so that he could get through the month.

For the past month, he has talked about the hotel. When he asks for it, we put the timer on for 20 minutes. When it goes off, we make him talk about five other things first. And then we talk about the hotel. How we will play on the waterslide. How we will eat cheeseburgers for supper. How we will sleep over afterward. What we will pack (primarily Big Tiger, Baby Tiger and Guy, his three favourite stuffies). And yesterday, IT HAPPENED. It happened exactly the way we planned it. He was on the waterslide for 4.5 hours. We walked to Wendy's for a cheeseburger. We put his buddies on the bed and we had a sleepover. Then this morning, we wake up. My eyes are red from the chlorinated air in the pool room. My stomach is bloated with grease. I'm tired after a night in an unfamiliar bed. But it was worth it. It was fun to work up to this moment, but now I need a quiet day to rest-up and recover. I smile at Noah and say good morning. He says, "Blue House." He says, "Blue House" as we pack our stuff and check-out. He says, "Blue House" as we drive home. He says, "Blue House" and then starts biting his hand and crying. We have been home for five minutes.

By the time the respite worker came, I was discouraged. We had discussed the Blue House and how it is ALL DONE. We talked about all of the fun things that are happening this summer. We made chocolate chip cookies as a diversion. This was going to be a high-energy day. The respite worker did some homework with him while I showered and started laundry. Then we had him work for a movie to shake him out of his obsession.

And so here I am in the lobby as back-up because it's a fragile day. The chance for more tears and biting are high. He's been out for two breaks already because it's hard to focus on the movie.

There are easy days. You just can't plan when they'll be. It seems, though, that it's never when you want them. After a hard day, you put the boy to bed and just start to relax with a cup of tea when friends come to your front door, asking if Noah's supposed to be on the roof. (That was the day he learned how to use the crankers for the windows. And also the day we started hiding the crankers). You pause to relax after two weeks of camping and suddenly your neighbour is shouting over the fence that Noah's by the river. There's no stored goodwill for the way you were alert and engaged for the previous two weeks. Each moment demands energy, attention, caution.

Very few moments are too difficult to manage. It's just that it's incessant. The relentless nature of autism is the Chinese water torture of parenting. It's not a bad life; it's just relentless. I'm still waiting to exhale.

DOG DAYS

We had the fire when Beau had been with us for eight months. We moved into a hotel for six weeks. Beau was farmed out to two different families for the daytime because he howled when left alone in the hotel room. We moved to a new house. We started a new school. Noah had meltdowns every day. And then one day we realized...
the dog was broken.

He was shivering with fear any time there was a loud noise. That year, Noah WAS a loud noise. Beau would lean against me or jump onto my lap and pant whenever Noah had a meltdown. If we were out walking and Noah got agitated, Beau would refuse to move forward. Instead of providing the support and service of a calm presence to help Noah, he was adding to the chaos.

The trainer came out from Ontario to help, but realized that Beau wasn't salvageable. Beau had PTSD. I think we all did. But, even as we were slowly emerging from the craziness of the last year, the dog was retreating more and more into his fear. We would need a replacement dog.

We held on for a few more months. We wanted to make it work. Then, one day when we were walking by the river,

Noah started to get riled up. I knew I had a limited amount of time to work him through his emotions before a total meltdown happened. I started contracting with him; "when we get home, we will play on the computer. You need a quiet voice now." Noah started to calm down, focused on getting home. The only glitch in my plan was that Beau had hunkered down, a nervous shivering mess. Panting and shaking. This I could not deal with. I let the leash go and continue on with Noah, hoping Beau will trail behind us. He doesn't.

He was stuck in the same place, getting smaller and smaller, as we walked on. I figured out a system of walking about 50 feet, making Noah sit down, running back to get Beau, bringing him almost to us and then leaving him while I moved Noah forward. It was the slowest-moving procession—a parade of jangled nerves and regret. I knew I wouldn't be able to make it home.

We finally made it to a friend's house—my main emergency contact. She also lives on our street and is first on my escape plan phone tree. Her friendly smile faded as she opened the door and watched my dignity crumble before her eyes as I tried to talk above the shouting boy and panting dog. "I need help with my special needs dog," I managed. Well, this was something she could handle. The last time I sent Noah over in this state, my house was on fire and she managed that whole scenario with style. This is small potatoes. A juice box is given, dog treats procured, and the four of us set out on our way, my friend walking Beau calmly ten feet behind us.

It became clear that, not only can Beau not function as a service dog, he couldn't even be considered a safe companion, unless I could afford a comforting dog-walker to accompany us on every outing. When Noah starts to get anxious, I don't need a seventy-pound trembling dog panting all over me. It wasn't a healthy environment for Beau either.

We reached out to our autism community and found a wonderful, gentle girl who was a good match for Beau. Her sister has a fluffy little dog, so Beau even gets his very own live stuffy to play with. We discussed with Noah what was going to happen, not knowing whether he understood any of it. The family took Beau home. We went away for the weekend, and arrived back on Sunday night to a quiet house.

We had spent three-and-a-half years waiting for a dog. One year enjoying him. One-and-a-half more trying to rehabilitate him. And now we've got nothing.

Well, that's not exactly true. We're down $24,000 and the six months Beau was with us in our brand new rebuilt home have made an indelible mark on our hardwood floors. It feels petty to think about the floors when we've lost a member of the family, but I feel raw and small inside and the scratches on the floor symbolize everything that's been lost. We've just been through a year in which we lost most of our possessions, now we've lost our dog, and the sparkle of what's new.

This began a year of breaking almost every dish that was saved and mistakenly giving away a box of treasures that had built-up over our first year. It seemed the universe was set on the idea of us losing absolutely everything but each other.

I grieved the poverty of a quiet house, the connections we used to make when strangers would see Noah and Beau working together, the goodwill that that image seemed to conjure from everybody. I grieved the fact that once again, I'm not living the happy ending that I so desperately want to be part of. I grieved for the way I apologetically let everyone who donated to the cause know that Beau was no longer with us. I grieved that Beau wasn't the miracle we were hoping for—the path into Noah's world.

The National Service Dogs Association promised though, that we could get a replacement dog if the first one didn't work out.

We get calls every spring and fall—each time a group graduates. No good matches. It seems that Noah is too autistic for a service dog, his behaviour is too out of control for them to entrust another of their dogs to us. It seems they bred the dogs to be super calm and gentle, but the result is that many of them are too sensitive to deal with anxiety. Predictably, I get my back up on these comments. Noah is not TOO autistic. He is exactly autistic enough to warrant us asking for help. I have challenged their breeding criteria—most people with autism have episodes of being loud and unpredictable. That needs to be a consideration for any dog planning to work with a child.

And yet, it hurts. It is hard to ask for help. It is hard to fail. I have watched the Dog Whisperer often enough to know that if there's a problem with a dog, the blame is usually placed on its owner. Instead of providing a service, this whole dog scenario has given me one more failure to carry.

It is November, and once again there are no matches for Noah. We request a companion dog instead. It would be good to have something to make-up for this part of our journey. I tell Noah that we might get another dog and his eyes light up. He says, "Yes I do!" Of course, he says that to a lot of things. We'll only know if it's a good idea once we get another one. I guess we'll wait until spring.

Ultimately all the things we hoped for are coming true. Noah hasn't escaped in the last year. He is able to walk with his class independently without anyone actively hanging on to him. And when I ask Noah if he wanted Beau to go to school with him, he said, "No, I want Sydney." Sydney is our beautiful, blonde eighteen-year old respite worker who is with him after school two days a week. "Given the choice between a service dog and a cute blonde, I'd make the same decision," says Noah's (male) EA. The boy is growing up.

THE VILLAGE

It took Noah to pull me into the world of autism. I did not come here willingly. My love for Noah made the trip possible, but without him I would have happily steered clear of this chaotic, loopy side of life. It's not that I was against disabled people in general; it was that people who were slightly different made me self-conscious. How do you have a conversation with someone who doesn't respond back according to the rules of etiquette? What if someone says something, but you don't understand his or her speech and you feel stupid? What if you end up looking weird? All sorts of questions kept me away from people who seemed "other," and the biggest concern of all of them was, "What about ME?" What if I am uncomfortable? What if I look awkward?" Me, me, me. That's the kind of girl I was. Not intentionally narcissistic, just self-conscious to the point of not being able to make space for others.

The people who work with Noah are not like me. They come to this planet willingly. They either have been born with some sort of strength of character that lets them think about others more than their own comfort, or are simply comfortable in their own skin and therefore at ease with others...or maybe they're just saints. I have no idea. I just know that they are better than me. They somehow know how to relate to Noah and to me without getting caught-up in their own egos and emotions. It's humbling. I want to dip each one of them in gold.

These are people who make barely more than minimum wage for the privilege of having their personal property damaged (see: various camera-related episodes), taking responsibility if things go terribly wrong (see: various news reports and 911 calls), and sharing in all sorts of nudity related stories (one has gotten to be very adept and diving to the bottom of the pool to retrieve swim trunks while at the same time hanging on to Noah's foot so his nudity remains undetected by the lifeguards). Right now my team consists of a self-proclaimed "tough cookie" who cried more than I did at Noah's grad, a hippy who started with us in grade eight and lets us be her second family even though her real family is astonishingly great, a gentle guy who is almost a foot shorter than Noah but who is completely unflappable and can get Noah to do anything, and a small blonde whose strength and maturity should no longer be surprising to me. I think that each of these people likes me, but they all love Noah. They are a big part of the village that has helped protect and shape him, and that has given him the skills and opportunities that he's needed to achieve the level of functioning he has.

There is no way to repay these people, or convey the gratitude I have for them. The biggest compliment I can give them is that my bunny, who is not especially known for etiquette or worrying about people's self-esteem, knows and recognizes each of them. Out of a sea of faces that do not matter to him (even if some of them SHOULD), these ones stand out. When I say their names or when they come to the door, Noah jumps up and grabs his shoes. He's been waiting for these ones. They're the ones who matter.

REACTIONS

Noah's been working all week delivering phone books. It's good work experience, plus the money raised from this job pays for a three-day camp his class attends in June— win/win. One day, he came by our house and was clearly in work mode. He said, "hi," but didn't stop or wonder if it was the end of the day. He ran back to the truck to get another book for the next house. His EA asked if I had noticed the police on the street earlier. I hadn't.

Apparently a neighbour down the street was scared to have a teenager come to the door and called the cops. Everything was worked out, but I was left wondering how I should be feeling. I never thought I'd see the day when my boy was independently delivering phone books, quickly moving from house to house. In the past, he would have tried to enter each house to see if anyone had left treats in the kitchen. (Believe me, Halloween used to be a huge time for meltdowns because Noah would get annoyed that I wouldn't let him go and explore each house and jump in each bed.) I never thought we'd get to this level of independence. In the past, he would probably have dropped the phone books and run to the river.

But we didn't teach him to avert his eyes when coming up the walk. He probably looked into a window on his way past, and that would be enough to scare someone.

As parents of autistic kids, we spend a lot of time defending ourselves from the reactions of others. We don't want our kids to be rejected, made fun of, bullied or misunderstood. We like t-shirts that say things like, "Keep staring, you might cure my autism. Then we can work on your social skills," or "I have autism—what's your excuse?" It's almost like we have to expect your negative response, and guard ourselves, and our kids against it before we even hear what you have to say.

And yes, sure, Noah has been the recipient of funny looks, ignorant comments and questions. And we've all heard nightmare stories of kids being bullied by other kids or tormented by their teachers or EAs. Overall though, I think people are pretty understanding. I just watched a show called something like, "What Would You Do?" where they set-up a potentially divisive situation and then record how unsuspecting people handle it. In this episode they chose a "family" of actors to go out for supper, with the teen boy playing a significantly affected autistic person. As he pretended to have a meltdown, nobody intervened. The producer finally had to call on the bully "plant," an actor who spoke all of the words we parents fear: "that kid is too loud, he's disrupting the place, you should keep him home." The unsuspecting diners all turned on this man and protected both the "autistic" boy and his family.

A similar thing has happened in our own family. When we were living at the hotel after the fire, David's in-laws came to visit. We were preparing to leave the next day to go to the cabin we rent every year. Because the summer had been so stressful and without routine, Noah was having a rough time and had become fixated on going to the cabin. That night at supper Noah started saying, "Cabin!" repeatedly, and even though we kept saying we were going, he had a meltdown. He screamed at the top of his voice and then started making a sound I can only describe as howling. The entire restaurant came to a standstill and I led the screaming boy and his shaking dog out as quickly as I could, leaving a wake of shock and awe behind us. After about fifteen minutes of screaming outside, Noah started calming down. Eventually we were able to go back inside, wash up and rejoin the family. All of us were humiliated and at a loss for words. Some people have no problem when their kids act up, but our whole family is not used to standing out or drawing attention to ourselves in this way. We are Mennonite—known as a quiet, peaceful, withdrawn kind of people. I am a performer, but that's very different. There is a line between stage and real life, and I would never sign-up for this kind of performance art. With as much dignity as we could muster, we finished our meal and retreated back to the safety of our room. We were at the hotel because of a trauma, but we knew everyone else was there on holiday, trying to have a break from reality, and we felt badly that a little too much reality accompanied us.

The next morning, when we went to pay for our breakfast, the front desk staff said that someone had paid for all six of us already and wished us the best. The judgment and condemnation we had heard in our own minds was brought low by this kind gesture.

We've also experienced the generosity and understanding of people when Noah really has been a threat—when he's jumped into danger and forced other people to get involved in his rescue, or when he went through his "break in" stage and went running into five different homes, respite workers, grandparents or parents trailing closely (but not closely enough!) behind. During these times, even when there might have been an initial sense of panic or judgment, there has always been an overlying sense of care for Noah's safety; a capacity to get over the initial feelings and understand that there is a bigger story involved.

I am beginning to understand that my fear of people's judgment says more about me than it does about other people. I fear rejection, and I am used to being in charge of Noah's wellbeing. I like the feeling of control, and there are so many things about autism that I cannot control, including how other people respond to it. The overwhelming evidence of people's capacity for empathy and compassion has challenged me. I have also seen, over time, that Noah can hold his own—some people will like him, others simply won't. And that's to be expected, if he is treated like I hope he will be—like anyone else. Whether or not people like him, or judge him, doesn't change his value. And if he doesn't care about other people's reactions, why should I?

BIG BROTHER

On Monday, I had booked a client, but forgot that David would be out of town. I was telling Jase that I'd need to get a respite worker to cover for the hour and he offered to take Noah. They'd go for a long walk to get ice cream. I asked if he felt safe doing it and he replied matter-of-factly, "Not completely, but I'll only get that through practice." We talked through a few scenarios and had Noah's tether belt on in case something did happen. (It goes around his waist and has a handle that comes down, so if he runs, you can grab the handle and he can't get away.) We told Noah about the plan. He thought it was great. (Anytime ice cream is involved, he thinks it's great.) So off they went, and I was able to go into my session with full concentration and no stress. But the minute the hour was up and my client left, I started panicking. I thought of all the things that could go wrong. I hated myself for putting Jase in a situation that was beyond him. I prayed that everything would be okay. I hyperventilated a little. Eventually I called my friend who lives down the road so I wouldn't have to be alone. In my mind's eye, I could see Noah dead and Jase unable to shake the responsibility for the rest of his life. How could I live with it? I stayed on the phone for twenty minutes until two handsome, beautiful teenagers wandered into view, walking side-by-side with no stress, no tension at all.

They had had a wonderful walk. Jase had stopped in at a shop on the way and Noah was patient. They'd had their ice cream and taken the long way home to make sure that the whole hour was passed. On the way, Noah started hunkering over and walking really weird and Jase asked him what he was doing. Noah said, "little." Jase didn't understand so Noah said, "small." So then Jase started hunkering over and walking really small too. Noah thought it was hilarious. Then he threw his hands up and shouted "big!" and Jase followed suit.

I can't tell you how happy this made me. It's so hard to find a moment like that with Noah—interactive and spontaneous. It makes you feel like a hero to get him laughing and be in on the joke with him. I'm so glad Jase had that. I like to think that the little/big comments were a recognition of sorts. Noah recognizing that he was walking with his big brother (the irony now that Noah is the taller of the two, making the little/big joke make sense). The first time that Noah had ever been out without an adult and things could not have gone better. The ease of their posture and the simplicity of the interaction painted a whole new picture in my mind's eye. Two guys enjoying each other's company. No weight to carry.

LETTING GO

You know how you can sit for so long in a position that you don't realize your leg has fallen asleep until you start moving? My body is tingling and I'm just realizing I've been holding a pose too long.

When I was pregnant, I was one of the most confident easy-going people ever. I read the books that said how perfect you have to be, how much you have to exercise, what kind of vitamins you should be taking. That seemed ridiculous to me. I was looking forward to this baby and knew that I had a generally balanced life. I didn't want to live with fear as my primary motivator. I had a very strong sense that everything was going to be fine. I loved kids. I was healthy. What could go wrong?

Noah's frequent escapes and brushes with death jolted me out of my confidence. Some people feel that my neuroses play a part in Noah's behaviour—if I could just learn to relax, he would show me that he was responsible, that he would come back when I called if I didn't physically retrieve him. But this is not a chicken-vs-egg-kind-of-thing. My fear is learned—a survival skill so I can continue parenting Noah. I came to it slowly, and it took a whole lot of out-of-control moments to change my posture into one of constant vigilance, my body frozen in "flight or fight" readiness.

Now I'm realizing (slowly, again) that it's time to move once more. My runaway bunny hasn't run for ten months now. It's not just that we haven't had to call 911. He is changing. Last week at Special Olympics, we were sitting in a circle listening to the coach. Noah said, "I want water" and when I said yes, he left the circle, ran 50 ft. over to where we had our stuff, grabbed his water bottle and ran back to the group. If your mind hasn't exploded over that last sentence, I obviously haven't communicated properly:

1. My non-verbal boy said a three word sentence
2. He waited for permission from me
3. He left and came back
4. At no time was anyone naked or in mortal danger

I need to let go of the death grip of worry that squeezes into my thoughts. I need to remember to exhale. I need to let my boy grow up and continue to change. He needs a different kind of parent again; one who trusts him and gives him the space to make decisions and take responsibility.

CAVE TROLL

I haven't been able to write in six months. Things have not been going well. My beautiful boy is drowning in anxiety and we are sinking with him. This is not like him. All of our energy is spent helping him cope.

When Noah was in full escape mode, I think I was more stressed than I am now, but I've never been more disheartened. He was doing so well last year. I thought we'd finally adjusted to this planet.

Now our world has become very small. Noah hasn't been able to attend church for the last five months. We can't have people over. I can't take him for a walk by myself because I will be overpowered. We're just splayed out on the carpet, practicing deep breathing and hoping the storm will pass. It's been a really long storm.

It is one thing to see your child struggle in the world and learn things more slowly than other kids; to accept that your relationship is not going to be what you had hoped for. But it's a different kind of awful to see the things that your child has get taken away. Noah's face has changed. His face is tense, his eyes reflect panic. There is a large hole and bruise on the palm of his hand from self-injury. He bites himself to manage stress. There are quite a few bruises and chiropractic adjustments for me as well. We have lost the spark of my sweet bunny.

All to say, this idea that Noah was getting easier, and it was going to be my chance to breathe, write, "find myself" and regain my inner mojo has been put on hold. It's all been too close to write about.

Parenting Noah is like caving. There are times of scrambling through narrow passes, times where the edges drop off perilously and a single miss-step could spell disaster, and other times when everything opens up into a beautiful otherworldly cathedral—when it's been worth the effort of navigating places few people have seen. The last six months have been a tight squeeze underwater, with only one nostril surfacing. Our focus is to keep moving, to not panic. We are hoping the tunnel will open up again soon; that we'll move into another beautiful space. Noah's moving into adulthood though, and I'm scared we're heading for a cave-in. If our support gave out, we'd be crushed. We're pretty crushed as it is.

Last week was a disaster. On Saturday, I took a professional development workshop at the monastery. When I came home, David and Jase were in tears and Noah was in the middle of a two-hour meltdown. David had already sedated him, so he was winding down, but he had bit his hand very badly and had also hurt David. Noah was shouting his list about the Blue House and banging on the wall.

When I talked to my mom that night, she indicated that she had felt physically unsafe at the sleepover the night before. Noah had grabbed her throat and squeezed, desperate for her to make sense of his list of words.

I felt responsible. It seems like some sort of chaos ensues whenever I go away. I was sorry I wasn't there to support Jase and David. I was scared for my mom, who is the only person who's ever volunteered to take Noah for a sleepover. When I wrote an email to my sisters, letting them know how bad it had gotten, I knew they'd also be concerned about Mom, and I was scared that they'd encourage her to stop taking him.

The following day, we had three people over for supper. In the past, this has worked out well. It's difficult to go to other people's house for dinner because it's harder to supervise him when he scampers off after eating (and awkward when you have to go running through parts of your friends' houses that they never intended for you to see). When we go over to someone's place for supper, we usually end the evening by thanking them and offering to replace whatever has been damaged. When we have people over at our place, we can let Noah go to the computer or his room, and it's pretty easy to visit.

Not this day.

Noah's meltdown from the day before had still not ended. Our friends came to the door to the sound of roaring. David took Noah to the other room while I got supper on the table, only to return a few minutes later wincing. Noah had tackled him and bit him in the chest. I left David to take care of the guests and tried to calm Noah down. I find it so hard to let people see this side of my bunny. I was mortified that people were witnessing him at his worst, and feeling sad and helpless seeing him struggle to cope with his anxiety and not succeeding.

Yet, we carried on. I emerged from the back room bruised and shaky, tears streaming, and politely asked if anyone wanted more wine. David and I spelled each other off until our respite worker showed up, trying to keep up conversation and make our guests feel safe and relaxed. It's not that we couldn't talk about what was going on, or that we were trying to hide it (though, if hiding it was an option, I'm sure I would have taken it). When you're in the tight part of the cave, the last thing you need is more people stuck in there with you. Autism can be a black hole that sucks up all the oxygen in the room, and sometimes I need friends who will open a door and let in a draft of fresh air. And, of course, that's what my friends did. None of them were shell-shocked. In fact, one of them was happy to have fodder for her own writing. They are all either very good actors, or a lot hardier than I give them credit for.

Why do I shy away from letting people in to the reality of my life? Why do I feel the need to apologize when people see Noah or me in a moment of weakness? Why does my own sense of inadequacy trump the capacity and compassion in other people?

Hmm. I'm starting to realize that "finding myself" might have more to do with these questions than with waiting for the cave to open up.

ADVENT

Since the day after Halloween, it looks like Christmas is here. The snow hasn't left the ground. The decorations are up and the Christmas medleys are fully-operational in the malls. At church, our priest desperately tries to keep us in Advent.

Advent is a season of waiting, of expectancy. It is the time of now, but not yet.

We are waiting.

We are waiting for Noah's anxiety to abate.

We are waiting for spring.

We are waiting for a new dog.

Some people in my family are waiting for Noah to be healed.

We make a calendar to show Noah what will happen. There will be no school soon. We will get to sing Christmas carols. We will drive to the airport to meet a new furry friend. The snow will go away.

Should we put "Goodbye Fear" on the calendar? Should we declare a day that Noah will learn to talk?

How do you differentiate between waiting and wishful thinking?

CHARLIE

We had almost given up on the idea of a dog. It's been almost a year since we said good-bye to Beau and we've moved on. When you live dog free for a year, you get used to a quiet house—to less vacuuming. Your nose gets over the indignity of sharing space with unexpected clouds of dog fart.

In mid-December we got a call. There was a dog. He had just barely failed the service dog training because he was a little too barky and exuberant. Did we want him?

We waffled again (we like waffles). We still had a lot of mixed feelings about the whole story. Could I be an alpha again? What if this dog also couldn't handle Noah? Why add to the chaos of our family?

And then we got an email with Charlie's picture.

I'm not a dog person. I don't believe in schmoozy things like love-at-first-sight (even though that's how I met my husband). I am not a person who spends time on the web looking at cute dog and kitten pictures.

Charlie was ours the minute we saw him. All bigheaded and regal, he was in a purple vest for his graduation picture—his shining moment before he failed to follow-through on his grad requirements.

It took a month to figure out how to get him to us (he was in Ontario and we're a province away. Airlines don't allow dogs to travel in luggage storage over Christmas and he was not a service dog, so he couldn't go in the passenger area.)

Is it fair to compare Charlie and Beau? One came loaded with expectation and rules. A service dog has a long list of do's and don'ts associated with it. It is going to be a miracle. It's going to be worth the long wait and thousands of dollars. It needs to bond with the special person. It's going to have to behave beautifully in public.

Charlie came when we had given up the expectation of even getting a dog. He's a consolation prize. He comes with no baggage—just his own tail, which he actually chases.

He can't go to school with Noah like Beau did, but he gets antsy at 2:45 every day, pacing by the front door. The big yellow school bus pulls up, I open the door and Charlie runs out to meet his boy. The bus driver, still hurting over the fact that he was never allowed to pet Beau, calls Charlie on to the bus for a quick hello. Then Noah walks to the house, dog jumping and leaping in circles around him. I don't know if Charlie is that bonded to Noah, or to the treat that accompanies this greeting, and I don't care. On days where Charlie misbehaves and runs off to catch-up on the pee happenings on the sidewalk, Noah is there to grab his collar and herd him back to the house. Look who's the responsible one now.

SPEAKING IN CODE

Although Noah has a vocabulary of over one hundred words and talks a lot at home, he's considered functionally non-verbal. His way of talking is to repeat a list of words over and over again. When he's having these "conversations" with you, he will lean in until your nose touches his nose to make sure you're listening. Usually it's a running monologue, though sometimes he needs you to respond. He often has a specific response in mind and it's hard to know what that is. I often manage by repeating what he last said, saying, "yes" or, lately, because of his anxiety, our most common responses are, "throw it in the garbage" (fear, winter—anything he doesn't like) or the cure all, "Noah is safe."

The term "functional" is a hard thing to define. When Noah first started speech therapy, we were asked what we wanted him to say. We taught him how to label all sorts of things to make his world less frustrating. We introduced a system called PECS (Picture Exchange Communication System) so he could point to pictures to make himself understood. We taught him scripts for safety reasons (so he could give his phone number and address) and for our own needs. One of my favourite scripts is:

K: Who loves you?
N: Mom and Dad
K: How much?
N: This much.
K: How much?
N: Right to the moon and back.
I don't know if this helps him in any way, but it sure makes my day.

Mostly we know what he wants. It's not too hard when your kid walks up to you holding a package of turkey franks and says, "THIS." Or throws a bag of Oreos in the shopping cart. Or tries to shoplift a DVD. The only difficulty in those scenarios is that, although we've taught him to use words to verbally request things (e.g. he holds up the wieners, I say "Mom, I want..." and he has to say, "Mom, I want wieners please" before he gets them), he doesn't have a lot of time for reasoning, deferred gratification or the word "no." A few months ago, he was adamantly asking for "Hawaii." Brilliant idea. However, not possible right now. I told him we don't have enough money to go. That didn't faze him at all. We were in the middle of a money program in therapy—teaching him how to label, identify and add up coins. He walked over to the change bucket, grabbed a handful of coins, put them in my hand and firmly repeated "Hawaii." Clearly he understood the problem and solved it. He never understands why we make things so complicated.

There are other times when it's harder to know what he's talking about. When he was in grade five, he was fixated on "Aimener." He asked for it constantly and we had no idea what it was. We googled it—nothing. We tried to ask him for details—is Aimener on TV? Is it a toy? A person? He was also into printing things on my computer, so we wondered if he meant "paper." This went on for months, not helped by the fact that Noah responds, "yes, I do" to just about any question.

Then, one day while I was cleaning around the TV, he got super excited. He grabbed an empty VHS cover and shouted "Aimener! Aimener!"

Aha. Aimener = "Are You My Neighbour?"—a Veggie Tales movie. As soon as we understood what he meant, we realized all the printing he had been doing was movie stills of the show, all taped in a cloud on the wall behind the TV. He must have thought we were idiots. Lovely people, those parents, but not so quick to catch on.

Lately, Noah has been more interested in communicating. It's one of the great joys of seeing him be more engaged in the world and empowered to make things happen. It is also one of the great frustrations for all of us because his ability to use language doesn't match his great ideas. Instead of a simple dialogue, our communication starts with a list of words followed by weeks or months of slow and persistent sleuthing to figure out what he means. One of his verbal lists right now is "train station, circle, circle, circle, circle, poster, big, Manitoba, red, red, yellow (list several colours), feet, blanket, fingers, building, mission, three." In addition to this word list, he has drawn over 500 versions of a picture of feet and a couple hundred pictures of trains. We understood what this meant fairly quickly: Noah wants us to buy the train station and replace the posters that they've taken down. Preferably, his favourite picture of feet would replace one of the posters.

How do we know this? We know he loves the foot picture— a friend of ours had it on her wall eight years ago, and he has loved it ever since. (Every single picture of her house has been cropped to the one place on the wall where that picture hung. The people in the supposed foreground of the picture are superfluous distractions.) A friend and fan of Noah's Art page on Facebook made two posters for him— one of the feet, one a collage of many of his versions of the same feet. Noah wants to drill holes on the corners of this poster so he can screw it on to the side of the building at the train station. He says, "circles" and points to the corners of the poster. He brings up handfuls of screws from the workshop several times a day. He Google Maps the train station and points to "building." Before we got the poster made, Noah had been trying to enlarge the picture of feet and print off small sections at a time. I got home from work one day to find he had printed over 50 pages of red and orange (the colour of the blanket in the picture) and was taping them together to create a gigantic version. In his verbal list, when he says all of the colours, I think he is seeing the picture broken into pixels and is listing them in order. "Mission," I think, refers to the fact that I've said we need permission from the train station. "Three" is his way of bargaining for how many posters we'll put up. He started with four, but has lowered his bid. "Manitoba" is one of the posters that used to be up. Actually, it was an Environment Canada sign that he got mixed-up with Manitoba Hydro.

The boy has dreams and schemes. He plans things on a macro scale. Now that he's communicated so clearly and patiently, he's waiting for us to make it happen. There is no discussion about who owns what building, what our yearly budget is for Staples, or what the significance of this project is. We try to meet him half way. David took him out to the train station with his poster and took pictures of him holding the poster in the right place. Our friend who made the poster Photoshopped a screen image of Google Maps with the "corrected" view including the foot picture. We have screwed the picture into his tree fort to make it seem like it's on a building. Noah has countered with suggestions that we put the picture on a billboard, preferably one with a large video display.

I always imagined that communication would be a simple exchange after school, talking about books and friends and feelings. Noah doesn't seem interested in any of those things. But the conversations we have now, usually accompanied with wild arm and body gestures, are better than I hoped for.

EPIPHANY ON THE TREADMILL

When the world is small, you have to be willing to take inspiration wherever you can find it. When Noah was little and I was battling depression, I lost my voice. I couldn't find the vocabulary I needed to articulate what was happening to me. There were some militant voices encouraging me to do whatever it took to make Noah recover. There were other pious voices talking about blessings. I was becoming friends with a mom whose child had Down's Syndrome and, when I tried to talk about my grief, she shut me down and told me I should just feel lucky that he was alive.

I needed to hear from strong, artistic, slightly crazy women who could face fear with love and curiosity. Trouble was, I couldn't fine those voices at that time in Winnipeg. Plus, I wasn't very good friend material, as getting dressed was often the biggest accomplishment of my day. The perfect solution was to find virtual friends in books.

Madeleine L'Engle and Annie Dillard became my dear friends; they helped me cobble together my own vocabulary. They reminded me that mothering is a big part of me, but not the only part. Neither of them are aware that I exist, so friendship might be a bit of a stretch to describe the relationship, but they've definitely been an inspiration.

Lately, my inspiration has been my treadmill. I'm still trying to shed my "grief baby"; the thirty pounds I've gained since Noah's diagnosis. I've tried running off and on over the last decade, but have had difficulty with injuries. We bought a treadmill a few months ago, partly for me and partly because we've noticed Noah's a happier camper if he runs at least 5K a day (which makes me wonder how we're related—5K is my personal Everest.)

I've learned a few things from the treadmill. The first is that I cannot multi-task. I was watching TV while jogging one day, when David came in to ask me something about childcare. When I realized I had forgotten to cover-off one event, I lost my balance, jumbled up my footing and went flying. We have now established the "Mom bubble"; when you see Mom on the treadmill, give her space. It seems I can't have both my body and my brain activated at the same time.

I have also learned, inadvertently, how to hurdle dogs. Charlie, panicked by his first time in a cone of shame (the plastic cone the vet puts on a dog after surgery so they don't disrupt the wound), had not been given the "Mom bubble" memo and jumped onto the treadmill while I was on it. For what? Comfort? Attention? I have no idea what the planned outcome was, but there was a sudden commotion of dog fur, legs, yelling, a graceless hurdle on my part and a very penitent denouement on Charlie's part.

From childhood, I've been taught what I should think and feel, and, as a control freak, I've suppressed a lot of my natural instincts. Nobody ever told me how my body should respond, though, and I've found that movement brings up feelings and thoughts in ways that I can't control.

121

It's become my most honest starting place, which is why most of my studies have centred on embodied spirituality.

As I've marched along on my treadmill, I've had vivid daydreams of being cast on the "Biggest Loser" and standing up to the trainer's bullying. I've processed the first year of having a service dog and those hours of "Walking Like an Alpha" that left me feeling depleted. The treadmill often leaves me feeling angry and inadequate. Whenever I get on there, my emotions start brewing.

Right after the terrible weekend when Noah was violent and we were so disheartened about the months of anxiety, I was on the treadmill listening to one of my favourite bands, "Of Monsters and Men." I wasn't paying attention to the lyrics until one line broke me open, "but we won't run, and we won't run, and we won't run." Not the most poetic phrase for sure, but I started sobbing and had to get off. I realized that running was a trigger for me. Every time I did heavy cardio, my body was transported back a few years to when I was running aimlessly along the river, trying to find Noah. The accelerated heart rate took me right into fight/flight mode and woke up the voice that screams inadequacy in my head. No wonder my previous attempts at running always resulted in injury and adrenal fatigue.

So... "we won't run." I needed permission to stop pushing myself. I got back on the treadmill, lowered the speed and marched along, forgiving myself for not running and allowing myself to find a new pace. I realized I needed to let go of feeling responsible for the previous weekend. As I walked, I felt myself move away from reactive mode. I wanted to learn how to separate myself from Noah, so that I could be responsive and empathetic without carrying his anxiety for him. I wanted to learn how to let people in to my life and not pretend to be strong.

I am still not running. Sometimes I saunter. Usually it's just a plain old chubby, middle-aged lady walk. I have to remind myself daily that this is kindness, not failure. The part of me that doesn't fit into last year's clothes wonders if I'll start running again, whether this is just a temporary phase. The part of me that is still trying to find words hangs on to the rest of that song, "Howling ghosts, they reappear in mountains that are stacked with fear, but you're a king and I'm a lion heart. A lion heart." I trudge on, feeling my courage grow.

ADVICE

Why is it that, within ten minutes of hearing that I'm the parent of an autistic child, people feel free to offer unsolicited advice? Do people think that I haven't spent the first fourteen years of Noah's life researching and trying different things? Do they assume a thousand other people haven't already told me about the miracles, the special diets, the supplements? What do they think I've been doing for the last decade-and-a-half? Peeling grapes and adjusting the cushions on my chaise?

Here's the thing—autism is complex. It does not honour the people doing research in the field, or the parents living through this, to casually blame all autism on McDonald's, vaccinations or the environment. I know many people who also grew up in the suburbs, eating their share of fast food who are up-to-date on their shots. Not all of them have autistic kids. Heck, I even only have one. It is a multi-faceted, complex, barely understood phenomenon. If you are a person who wants to connect with a person who is parenting someone with autism, why not start with a question? Chances are, that person may already have some ideas of how they think about autism. They've also probably tried some things. They may be still hoping for a cure, or they may be adamant that their child deserves unreserved acceptance. You won't know unless you ask.

I was told in a thirty-minute conversation, that I should read a specific book, consider going gluten-free, change schools, reconsider our commitment to having Noah run on an indoor track and blame genetically modified food for his diagnosis. I was also asked to disclose how "well" my other son copes with his brother and told a story of one sibling who is the best friend to his autistic brother, who only sees him as gift and who seems to radiate healing energy.

I try to receive all of this in the spirit that it's given. The underlying text is care for my child, a desire to lessen the impact of autism in our family's life and to provide encouragement.

But here's the thing. Living with autism is actually pretty tiring. I have tried many different methods of helping. I have also felt the oppressive weight that I have not tried hard enough—there is always something more that I could do. I also wrestle with the costs of many interventions—not just financially, but the time and energetic toll that they take on our family (You try feeding ten golf ball-sized, compost-tasting vitamins to a child who already has eating issues.) When you're eating seaweed and forty supplements for supper, you've got to question the quality of life. When we were on a severely restricted diet, Noah would get a rice cake and a glass of water at school when the other kids would bring cupcakes into the class. I mean, come on. As socially isolating as autism is, do we need one more thing that tags us as different, as hard to include?

Having Noah run makes a difference to the anxiety levels he lives with. And, instead of beating myself up that I can't run 5K or that I hate the cold, we bought a treadmill so at least we get some running time for him through the winter.

Is it as ideal as running outside? Maybe not. But is it better than a kick in the pants? Why, yes. Yes it is. There's no need to talk about the environmental damage my treadmill creates in this example. But perhaps there could be a small "hurray" that we've found something that works.

So, to those of you that need to offer advice, I come in peace. I know you want me to know that you care and want to relate to my story. I know you want to be helpful. Please just stop with the suggestions and offer encouragement instead. Be curious. See that we're trying to fit in and don't focus on how different we are or how difficult our lives must be. Just respect us. I am more than willing to accept responsibility for my child's autism, but I will not accept the blame.

BREAKTHROUGH

The anxiety has broken, thanks be to God. We are all still a little shaky, a little disoriented, but the worst is over. After a steady build over eight months, we had an "anxiety cleanse," which made way for a wonderful breakthrough. You know how New Year's starts with a pledge to new health and fitness, and you go off all sugar and caffeine and start working-out, but then end up with a migraine, hanging over the toilet? All of the crap, the toxins, the body's addiction to sugar—all of it needs to move through the system before you start feeling better. (That's hypothetical—I feel better as soon as the coffee starts flowing again, personally.) Last month was our anxiety cleanse. Apparently, we needed to barf out all the leftover bits of worry and trauma before we could move on.

I didn't know why the anxiety started. It seemed to be a significant force in July, after Noah's first week at day-camp. He had never been before, and it seemed like a good idea at the time. The camp had twenty-five kids and twenty-five counselors, all lovely people. However, they had a model that was not a 1-1 match-up. All the counselors got to know all the kids. In theory, that's great, but Noah had no "go to" person who knew and understood him. On his second day, no one remembered to reapply sunscreen in the afternoon and he came home badly burned. He had never had a sunburn before and thought he was dying. He drew lots of pictures of himself glowing red and looking miserable. We had to keep cool cloths on him to get him to sleep and gave him Advil. Four days later, when his skin started peeling off, he was very concerned. You try describing to a nonverbal person that skin falling off is normal and that you will not end up with your innards falling out. It reminded me of the first tooth he lost—a very perplexing and scary phenomena when you randomly lose body parts.

It also didn't help that the camp counselors didn't know how to respond to Noah's verbal lists. We try to be pretty consistent with how we respond so that we don't inadvertently feed the behaviour, but it's hard to maintain consistency with twenty-five people. After camp, we went on our big trip to Europe and Noah struggled more than usual with everything. We gave him a recipe card that said, "I am OK" on it and he clutched it through Rome until it disintegrated in the heat and sweat.

On our way home, he had a spectacular meltdown just as we were getting our boarding passes at SwissAir. We had to sedate him and ensure he was calm for half an hour before they'd let us on the plane. Of the many understanding reactions we've had to Noah, most people are not too excited to get in a confined space a thousand feet in the air with any kind of explosive, our boy included.

We got back from our trip and into school three days after everyone else had started. We found out that Noah's EA was not going to be with him that year (he was only working two days a week and the teacher thought an inconsistent schedule would be harder than getting used to a new person). We got a new EA who was, again, a lovely person, but didn't know Noah and didn't know anything about sports or computers.

Somewhere in that time, we lost our bunny and got a very tense, angry, anxious boy in his place. He injured the EA. We had meetings at school. I argued passionately to try medical marijuana to help with his agitation. The only other time that Noah had been so out of sorts was the year after the fire, when we were trying all kinds of anti-anxiety meds and they were making him crazy or leading to seizures, so I was very afraid to medicate him again. We got the old EA back two days a week and the school hired his EA from elementary school for the other three days. He injured her and had to be held down by four people before they could move him to the quiet room (it wasn't so quiet when he was in there). We stopped going to church. Stopped having people over.

At the same time, Noah started drawing several hundred pictures of himself on a bed. His one leg was a different colour than the other. His accompanying verbal list was "danger, hospital, loud, colours, dark." It became clear over time that he was processing his accident when he was eight. He would draw himself on the hospital bed and draw black lines over the parts that hurt: head, leg, stomach.

We had never really processed his accident. It changed him. He didn't bolt after that except a brief, one-month bolting spree on the one-year anniversary after the fire. He seemed to be more aware of us, trusting our intentions to help him. We've been so busy dealing with the autism that it's hard to remember that Noah was significantly traumatized by the accident itself with no ability to talk through the experience.

One way we've tried to help with this is through Body Talk. It's a holistic, non-invasive therapy that doesn't require someone to talk. I take him once a month and we've been going for a year-and-a-half. In the session the month of the "anxiety cleanse," Noah started talking more than he ever had. His verbal list started with the hospital, but he added "car, lights, sign, raining, red, blue, horn, loud." It was raining when the accident happened, and he was running to the Robin's Donut sign. The red and blue lights seemed to be the flashing lights of the ambulance—also very loud. Then he said "ouch" and pointed to his head, stomach and leg. (This is not what Body Talk usually looks like, by the way. The therapist was working on fear, but the words were really unexpected.) Then Noah pointed to the table he was on and said, "bed." I think he meant stretcher. He showed us that he had to wear a mask and a collar (by gesture). Then he said, "Scared, help me."

The biggest memory I had of his accident was how he responded to me in emergency. It was my first experience of being recognized and needed. Looking back, it makes sense that the anxiety he felt at camp feeling physically in danger with the sunburn and not having a specific person to turn to triggered the feeling he had in the emergency ward of realizing that he was alone and in danger.

I moved into the same position I had been in seven years ago—standing by his head, looking down and stroking his hair. I told him that he was safe. That Mom was there. His eyes locked on mine and he made the most intense eye contact that I've seen. When he was three, we'd spend hours in ABA therapy teaching him to look into our eyes and for every three seconds, he'd get a gummi bear. Now he was looking at me for full minutes at a time.

He touched his sternum and said, "Little Noah." I patted the same area and said, "Little Noah is safe." Somehow, in all of that, the fever broke.

It's been over a month now since the breakthrough. Noah is still more anxious than he used to be. One of his favourite verbal lists right now is "Noah is safe, breathe, relax, chill." We still start some days with belly breathing on the carpet before we can focus enough to eat breakfast, get ready for the bus. His hand has healed though, and I can take him for walks with Charlie without feeling scared. David and Jase were out of town a few weeks ago, so Noah,

Mom and I all went to a restaurant for noodles. Nothing happened. It was fantastic.

It's been a slow emergence from the anxiety squeeze. It's been contagious – I've never struggled with anxiety before and I had a full on panic attack on laundry day. Something smelled hot and I thought there was a fire. I had to call David to come home and make sure. It was mortifying. My biggest fear was not that the house would burn down again, it was that it would burn on my watch again. If David was home, we could both take the blame. That is my trauma, the one that still has a squeeze on me.

It's like we just had an overwhelming guest stay with us for too long. At first, we tried to make a place for the anxiety, then it became a bully. As we were handing out an eviction notice, it trashed the place. Now it's gone, but there is clean up to do and we've taken on a few of its mannerisms. All I want for summer is a fresh slate of guests: hope, peace and joy.

AUTISM AWARENESS DAY

It is Autism Awareness Day, ironically the day right after April Fool's Day. Yesterday, the joke was on you. Today, there is nothing funny to explain why one out of every eighty-eight kids is wired wrong.

The theme for today is "Light it up Blue." Everyone in the autism community buys blue light bulbs to light up their houses. Several national monuments get lit up in blue as well. I guess it helps us remember that we're not alone. You drive around town, dismayed by all of these blue lights, calling out like mini-lighthouses—Beware! Rocky shores ahead! The symbol is also to demonstrate that we're awash in blue. Everyone is affected in some way by autism. One out of eighty-eight means that if it's not in your family, chances are it's in the family of someone at your work, or your school. Even if you don't know somebody, you might be affected by it. There is a woman in Winnipeg who probably still remembers the feel of my boy's body hitting her vehicle—her life jarred by the reality of autism. There are several people in the city that may think of my boy on this day, remembering their acts of heroism and quick thinking that were a part of one of our rescue stories. There are probably a few politicians and school trustees who take a moment on this day to silently wish that autism and the funding issues and feisty parents that go along with them never existed.

More than likely though, a lot of this "Light it up Blue" campaign has to do with profit and finding one more way of splitting parents of autistic kids from their money. It's kind of like the pink campaign for breast cancer—a once nice idea that has become a monster in terms of finding the profit of marketing to special groups.

Finances aside, the big push today is on building awareness for autism. This is why I go a bit off on days like this. I mean really. Do we need to become MORE aware of autism? Because I feel pretty aware. And the issue I have with the world is not about awareness. I've been on the receiving end of warm understanding, and people seem pretty aware of that diagnosis when they're encountering my bunny.

This is what I propose: On April 2nd, can we make two promises?

First, that we won't pity people with autism or parents of those people. Because pity is the twin sister of hatred. It keeps a wedge between us and, trust me, it doesn't help you see the beauty and gift that each person with autism has to offer and it doesn't dignify that person or their parents. Curiosity, care and enjoyment might be better ways to go.

Second, could we declare April 2nd to be one day where we don't talk about cures, vaccines, miracles or supplements? We just need one day when other people can simply accept the fact that autism exists and that the first goal should not be about how to eradicate it. As Temple Grandin, chief spokesperson for autistic people everywhere, suggests, without autism, there would be no electricity, no computers, no brilliant mathematicians or artists. Without autism, we'd be one big episode of Big Brother, where all people do is play a social game and not accomplish anything. So instead of trying to vilify autism and suggest ways that I can work harder at curing my child, would you instead like to buy my kid a Slurpee or take him out for a cheeseburger or (if you're too scared to spend time with him) buy a gift to celebrate a parent or person who works with autistic people?

The promise I can make in return is to remember that Autism isn't the only thing I need to be aware of. Even though my world is coloured by this particular word, I can promise to remember that you may have a word that colours your world, and I will try to be curious and caring about that.

THE COST OF AUTISM

In terms of cost analysis, autism is a rich person's game. To support Noah, we've bought and replaced many cameras. We've bought hundreds of toys, looking for the elusive one that would capture his interest. I've had to replace my iPod (I'm going to give half the blame for that one to David since it was his brilliant idea to "save" it by putting it in the oven after Noah demonstrated his displeasure at a song by throwing it in the fountain.) We had to buy an industrial strength trampoline after the Wal-Mart one gave in to the pressures of over-exuberant jumping. We've spent thousands of dollars over the years on supplements, speech therapy, ABA consultants, and educational devices. And, of course, we had to replace the house. So there's that.

But there are other costs involved too. Yes, autism has taught us about beauty, humility, community and how to be human. We wouldn't trade our bunny or our story for anything. But we have paid a price.

I've paid with my body. I can't put all of the blame for my weight gain on autism (though I'm happy to give it its fair due), but I also have occasional bruises and bites, a body tired after years of intense stress, and sensitive adrenal glands. My hair started turning grey the year after the fire.

If I don't work hard at processing my emotions and releasing them (along with stress), I find it easy for depression to take over.

I've paid by choosing a smaller world. Noah's planet is hard to get to. I've chosen to let go of some things that I wanted because it's too hard to invest in both his world and mine. So, although I ran a dance company before the diagnosis, and although I have a masters degree and share many of the same skills as my husband, I haven't been able to have a job that would provide security, benefits, social interaction, or a sense of identity. I was okay sacrificing some of that when the boys were young and Noah was doing therapy at home, but I always thought I would be able to return to the work world once he was in school. Because the parent-run lunch program wouldn't take him, though, I had to pick him up from 12-1pm every day in elementary. Now he stays at school through lunch, but comes home at 2:45pm. There isn't a daycare for people over the age of eleven who need support, so someone has to be home on days when there is no school, early dismissal, summer vacation. Respite has allowed me to work part time, but there is a limit to what I can do, and what kind of job offers that flexibility. I thought I would be one of those people who would Contribute To The World and Make a Difference. I thought I'd have a far reach. Instead, I've made a big difference to Noah's world and I've contributed to the field of autism.

We just celebrated the 20th anniversary of the dance school I founded. I had been asked to choreograph a production number with alumni dancers and it was so much fun. The physicality of it, the laughter and stories shared with my former dancers, the fun of creating and performing again, seeing the girls I taught become beautiful extraordinary women—it was all so fabulous. And then, of course, the costumes, the lights, the performing, the applause—I ate it all up, satisfying a craving I'd neglected for years. Heck, it was just fun to be in a room where everybody could talk and not a single person said, "blue house" once.

When it was over, I felt the weight of that diagnosis. It is too simple to say that autism was the only thing that took me away from that life. I have performed since then. But living with autism requires a lot of creativity and energy. I don't always have enough to feed it and my own needs.

I want to live with a sense of abundance rather than scarcity. I want to believe that time and energy aren't bound. I see glimpses of this being true.

Every week in church, our closing prayer begins with "Glory to God, whose power working in us can do infinitely more than we can ask or imagine." I imagine I'm still asking for the wrong things, because I'm still often stuck in seeing what's undone right in front of me, let alone MORE than what I can ask or imagine.

So, yes, the journey has been valuable. Noah is a gift. All is well. And the cost has been high.

WHAT AUTISM HAS GIVEN ME

When Noah was first diagnosed, people said it was a blessing; that I would change and become a better person, that I would grow closer to God. I rejected those words at the time—if I could trade the gifts of autism for an untempered life I would have, no question. But a trade was never offered, and over the years I have come to begrudgingly receive the gifts of autism.

Autism has shown me the beauty of grey. In a culture of simplistic formulas and black and white thinking, autism has forced me into an appreciation of complexity and subtlety. There is no one cause, no single cure, no "right" way to parent a child. There is no easy benchmark to work toward to judge success. A superficial understanding of God cannot stretch far enough to hold the amount of pain and questioning that autism brings. It must expand and, in the expansion, it becomes deeper, richer and more compelling. More like actual nourishment than superstition. It seats you on the side of people in the margins, and you learn to build up the muscle of compassion.

Autism has taught me humility. I've been naked in public, both literally and figuratively, many times. I've been found lacking in my ability to keep Noah safe, quiet and out of harm's way. I, who have tried to be responsible, to be autonomous, have found that I cannot shoulder the burden myself. And it's taken years of shame and feeling like a failure for me to look up and realize that nobody is asking me to do it on my own. I'm humbled by the concern instead of judgment that I see in people's eyes when Noah is having a meltdown, and by the concern of his school and respite teams when he's not himself. Slowly but surely, autism is helping me learn one of the hardest skills of being human—how to receive.

Autism has taught me about gratitude. It was so hard to give up the idea that happiness would come through success, the avoidance of pain or simply by living long and prospering. Every day that we're alive is good. And when we die, it will have been worth being alive. I have learned to appreciate the beauty of an exit sign, our favourite tree in the park, the longevity of Baby Tiger, and the beautiful purring dolphin noise that Noah makes when he is happy. Henry David Thoreau said, "It's not what you look at that matters, it's what you see." Autism has changed the way I see.

Autism has helped me get over myself. This coming from a woman who was born for the stage. Learning to sit on the sidelines has been painful, but it's also given me a view of myself as part of a beautiful inter-connected web instead of at the centre of a tedious melodrama. As I've let go of self-consciousness and my own ego, I've found a bit more space to take in other people and not hold on to my own feelings and wounds quite as tightly.

Most importantly, living with someone with a profound disability has taught me what it is to be human. My love for Noah is not dependent on his ability to speak. I get frustrated when I can't communicate with him clearly, and I wish I understood him better, but I don't love him any less. This has helped me realize that that's true in my life too. People don't love me because I'm perfect. My flaws don't get in the way of other people's love for me. The only thing that interferes is my inability to receive that love. Brené Brown says, "You are imperfect. You are hard-wired for struggle. And you are worthy of love." Loving Noah has taught me that I am worthy of love too. I cannot earn it. Nor am I asked to.

CONCLUSION

This morning, the dog exploded and there is diarrhea all over my office and the dining room floor.

Jase is sick, wrapped in a blanket and trying to keep down a bowl of chicken noodle soup (the dog smells are not helping this endeavor).

Noah is running through the house alternating between two verbal loops, "Goodbye Fear! Return to sender with consciousness!" and "Noah is safe," a mongrel mix of therapy, yoga, Body Talk, working out old traumas and apparently the need to give the people at school one more reason to think our family is weird. Why doesn't my kid just stick to, "To infinity and beyond!," the universal phrase of choice for people with autism?

We have been getting up early every day this week. CBC radio was going to feature Noah's art on the morning show, but his story keeps getting bumped by More Important News.

I am packing up to spend another day writing. I have done this for three days this week, needing to rediscover my momentum and find my voice again after six months of radio silence.

My cell phone is on, but nothing terrible has happened all week.

It's April and there's still snow on the ground. I'm ready for spring. The winter has been too long.

To see Noah's artwork and cards, look for "Noah's Art Winnipeg" on Etsy or Facebook.

Kalyn's website is www.kalynfalk.com.

For more information on Autism, a helpful resource is www.asatonline.org.

To find out more about Kelley Jo Burke (relentless), please see www.kjb.squarespace.com.

ABOUT THE AUTHOR

Kalyn Falk, MA, is a spiritual director, workshop facilitator and retreat guide. She was the Parent Support Network Coordinator for MFEAT (Manitoba Families for Effective Autism Treatment) and writes in the areas of both spirituality and autism. She has been shaped significantly by parenting two amazing boys, one of whom is profoundly autistic. (The other is a profound hipster.) Kalyn lives in Winnipeg, MB, Canada with her boys, her husband David, and her service dog dropout, Charlie.

Made in the USA
Charleston, SC
11 November 2013